THE REALMS OF ARTHUR

Helen Hill Miller

THE REALMS OF
ARTHUR

PETER DAVIES · London

First published in Great Britain 1970

432 09395 8

Printed in Great Britain by Fletcher & Son Ltd, Norwich

ACKNOWLEDGMENTS

Grateful acknowledgment is made to the following copyright owners for permission to quote as indicated:

Appleton-Century-Crofts, *Arthur King of Britain* edited by Richard L. Brengle (copyright © 1964 by Meredith Publishing Company); Barnes & Noble, Inc., *Speculum Historiale;* The British Museum, *The Sutton Hoo Burial* by R. L. S. Bruce Mitford; Jonathan Cape, Ltd. (London) and the Estate of H. E. Butler: *The Autobiography of Giraldus Cambrensis* translated from the Latin and edited by H. E. Butler; J. M. Dent & Sons, Ltd. (London) and E. P. Dutton & Co., Inc.: *The History of The Holy Grail* Sebastian Evans, 1899; *The Mabinogion* ed. Jones, Everyman's Library; *Le Morte d'Arthur,* Malory, Everyman's Library; *Arthurian Chronicles,* Wace and Layamon, Everyman's Library; Harvard University Press, Tacitus *Agricola,* Diodorus Siculus *Bibliotheca Historica,* Procopius *History of the Wars,* Loeb Classical Library; Michael G. Jarrett and Brian Dobson *Britain and Rome,* Essays presented to Eric Birley, 1965; John R. Morris *Surrey Archaeological Collections* Vol. LVI, 1959; Thomas Nelson & Sons, Ltd. (London) *Roman Britain and Early England* 55 B.C.–871 A.D. Peter Hunt Blair, 1963; Longmans Green, Ltd. (London) and W. W. Norton & Co., Inc., *Sir Gawain and the Green Knight* tr. Marie Boroff 1967; Oxford University Press, New York and Associated Book Publishers, Ltd. (London): *English Historical Documents,* Vol. I, ed. Dorothy Whitelock, General Editor David C. Douglas; Penguin Books, Ltd. (London), Caesar: *The Conquest of Gaul* tr. S. A. Handford; Geoffrey of Monmouth: *The History of the Kings of Britain* modern version by Lewis Thorpe; Sidgwick & Jackson, Ltd. (London), *Arthur of Britain,* E. K. Chambers, 1927; The Society for Promoting Christian Knowledge, Nennius: *History of the Britons* by A. W. Wade-Evans, 1938; University of Wales, *Trioedd Ynys Prydein* tr. Rachel Bromwich

MAPS BY RAFAEL PALACIOS

CONTENTS

I	FOREWORD: MATTER OF BRITAIN	9
II	THE ROMANO-BRITISH SOCIETY	29
III	DARK AGE DUX BELLORUM	67
IV	CELTIC ORIGINS	99
V	THE ARTHUR OF CHRONICLE	123
VI	PROFESSIONAL TOUCHES	145
VII	THE GLASTONBURY FABLES	165
VIII	REPATRIATION OF THE LEGENDS	191
IX	AFTERWORD: DARK AGE HEROES	209

APPENDICES and INDEX: *215*

    A.   *List of Illustrations*   *217*

          Maps   *221*

    B.   *Sources of quotations not identified in the text*   *223*

    C.   *Brief Bibliography*   *225*

          Index   *231*

FOREWORD 1

MATTER
OF
BRITAIN

ALMOST 1500 YEARS AFTER ARTHUR LIVED, HIS LEGEND IS A living part of the Western heritage.

Throughout the Western world, the holding of 'round tables' is an accepted feature of organizational life, from corporations to churches to universities. Internationally dignified by Latin, exceptionally gifted intellectuals gather at sessions of *Mensa Rotunda*.

Readers of comic strips, intellectual and otherwise, look forward to Harold R. Foster's Sunday episodes of *Prince Valiant in the Days of King Arthur*.

As this book was being finished, *Camelot* was showing at first-run movie houses in the United States from coast to coast. A Hollywood version of the love triangle of Arthur, Lancelot and Guenevere, it flaunted an Irish and an Italian actor and an English actress in glorious technicolor; but the names are there. The film is based on the musical of the same name, which in turn is based on the book of the English author, T. H. White, *The Once and Future King.*

The musical opened in New York in the winter of 1960. Before it moved on to London, a long run, a travelling company, and imposing record sales made its tunes so familiar that after the assassination of John F. Kennedy a verse from its theme song was written into political history:

> *Don't let it be forgot*
> *That once there was a spot*
> *For one brief shining moment*
> *That was known as Camelot.**

> * Copyright © 1960 by Alan J. Lerner & Frederick Loewe, used by permission of Chappell & Co. Inc. New York

Previously, President Kennedy's chairman of the Federal Communications Commission, when he described the culture of commercial television as a 'waste land', had echoed the title of T. S. Eliot's bitter poem expressing Western agony of spirit in the years just after World War I; the Arthurian reference is to the blighted and sterile realm of the Maimed King whom a Grail knight alone can heal.

In the summer of 1967, the story of the Maimed King was given fresh presentation in the Bayreuth Music Festival's new mounting of Wagner's final opera, *Parsifal.* The themes of the prelude—the Eucharist, the lance, the Grail and the triumph of faith—explain why the composer called it a "consecrational festival play." He intended it for performance only at Bayreuth, but over the opposition of his widow, the Metropolitan Opera Company was performing it in New York by the early 1900's.

Like *Parsifal,* the currently most familiar versions of the story in English are those produced during the 19th century revival of the idylls of the king; Arthur's noble purposes well served the Victorian morality of art. The middle-aged among English-speaking peoples, therefore, usually think of Arthur and his companions as presented

1 1

in pasteurized children's versions by Howard Pyle, and given the strength of ten in college literature courses—though in accompanying illustrations by Burne-Jones, William Morris or Aubrey Beardsley these knights are apt to appear as delicate creatures much given to palely wandering.

To the indoctrinated who like to keep their youthful illusions whole, with the implacable accuracy of a child who can bear no departure from the familiar sequence of a story, my foreword is not an invitation. In this book, Arthur's story is not the same from chapter to chapter, and frequently it bears small resemblance to the one the 19th century Romantics told. The realms of Arthur are many, and they differ from time to time and from place to place. My purpose is to explore the origin of Arthur's enduring charisma in a rough Celtic setting of around the year 500 A.D., and to record its changes over the succeeding centuries through medieval times.

Merlin, the skillful shape-changer, never contrived a more striking transformation than that of Arthur, rough and ready military commander in Celtic Britain during the Dark Age of scant record after Rome abandoned its province of Britannia, into Arthur, king of a medieval court in Never-Never land, known throughout all Christendom as the model of knightly courtesy. It is indeed strange that a 5th century British warrior, leader of semi-civilized Britons against semi-civilized Saxons, emerged as such a king.

Accounts of his exploits, passed on by word-of-mouth for half a millennium, reached the medieval world through folk-memory, oral tradition and fragments of early chronicle. Then they began to be written down, and in the 12th century, on the Continent, they suddenly acquired literary form.

The spread of the medieval versions was phenomenal. Seven hundred years after Arthur's time, he and his companions peopled heroic tales in castle and camp from the coasts of Wales to Crusader outposts on the shores of the eastern Mediterranean.

By the mid-13th century, Jean Bodel of Arras, poet and Crusader who originated the phrase, Matter of Britain, to describe the Arthurian cycle, could say that there were only three matters worthy of a story-teller's attention: the matter of the ancient world—epics of the Trojan War and Aeneas, of Alexander and Constantine; the matter of France —tales of Charlemagne and his knights; and the matter of Britain— stories of Arthur and his Round Table.

> *Ne sont que. iii. matieres à nul home attandant:*
> *De France et de Bretaigne et de Rome la grant;*
> *Et de ces. iij. matieres n'i a nule samblant.*
> *Li conte de Bretaigne sone si vain et plaisant;*
> *Cil de Rome sont sage et de san aprenant*
> *Cil de France de voir chascun jor apparant.*

During the two hundred years between 1300 and 1500, brilliant miniatures of Arthurian exploits illumined the vellum pages of patient clerkly copiers of manuscripts for noble and royal libraries. Sculptors, wood-carvers, fresco-painters, tile-makers portrayed them from Cologne

and Regensbruck to Modena and Otranto; from Chertsey-on-Thames to Paris and Palermo. Usually their scenes depicted specific incidents in the best-known stories; sometimes their subjects were simply the favorite sports and pastimes of the medieval world, from falconry to tournaments.

In the early 14th century, Jacques de Longuyon invented the first of a succession of popular lists of Nine Worthies—three great conquerors of antiquity, three great Jews, three great Christians. Then and subsequently, Arthur is one of the three great Christians, whether in the words of Welsh triads, in the stained glass of St. Mary's Hall, Coventry, or in tapestries such as the late 14th century masterpiece from the Paris workshops of Nicholas Bataille, now in the Cloisters of the Metropolitan Museum of New York.

Tracing the sources of such an expanding charisma is absorbing; tracing its factual basis more absorbing still.

What is the evidence for an historic Arthur? Or was his a name of a fictitious hero that gathered into one the more memorable exploits of many men?

Where did he live? Did he ever use the Iron Age fort at South Cadbury in Somerset that tradition has called Camelot?

Where did he die? Can the site of Camlann, where Arthur's and Modred's forces met in a battle fatal to both, be located now?

Where did Arthur fight the series of engagements that made his fame as a war leader? Or is this list a collection of the names of well-remembered victories achieved by a number of commanders over a considerable time? In particular, where was the Mons Badonicus where Romano-British forces won not a battle but a war?

When beginning a search for answers, it is worth noting that all three of Jean Bodel's 'matters' originate in Dark Ages, periods of plentiful legend and sparse record—but also periods into which contemporary archaeology is just now letting light.

Today, exploration of Arthurian geography can be undertaken with a text—literary or historical—in one hand, and the findings of an archaeological research team in the other, and it is thus that the present reportage took place.

The texts date from intervals over a span of 1500 years; exceptionally, Britain's Dark Age centuries are bounded by written record on both sides. Caesar's *Commentaries* describe the tribal structure of the island as it was at the time of his two reconnaissances-in-force in 55 and 54 B.C.; it became the enduring basis of administration under Roman rule and was the island's remaining political resource thereafter. Tacitus's *Annals* narrate the Roman invasion in 43 A.D. by

which Claudius initiated a lasting occupation; his *Agricola* details the subsequent campaigns in Scotland of his famous father-in-law. The way of life thereafter established while Britain was a province of Rome was the way of life the Romano-Britons of Arthur's time fought to defend. It lasted nearly half a millennium.

By the early 5th century, reliable record has become very scanty; the deficiency endures until after a new conquest established Anglo-Saxon rulers in various parts of the island and King Alfred consolidated these holdings in a unified English rule. With the 9th century, history again becomes available in the *Anglo-Saxon Chronicle*.

In the obscure years—and these were Arthur's years—there is a serious gap. Yet archaeologists and historians, feeling their way in the darkness, are finding an increasing number of fragments within their reach, hard chunks about whose reality there can be no question, though views may differ about the places into which they fit.

Part of the new evidence comes from sifting large masses of earth, part from sorting small mentions in manuscript. The earth-sifting of modern archaeology, with its geophysical devices to aid selection of likely spots in which to dig, and its recent accumulation of greatly expanded experience in the interpretation of finds, is showing what groups, if not what individuals, occupied significant areas, and, within narrowing limits, when they were present there. Whether directed to massive dykes or delicate grave goods, current exploration is dating or locating evidence that fills in the narrative. The recent spread to the Continent of the search for both artifacts and records relevant to Britain has brought archaeologists to sites that illuminate migration; historians, collating records from Brittany to Constantinople, are widening the number of early memories and interpretations of what happened then. And the perennial prospect and occasional appearance of fortuitous contributions, from chance finds in the earth to sudden identifications of neglected manuscripts, continually tantalize hard-working specialists and occasionally put within their grasp pots of gold no longer at the end of the rainbow.

16   The initial problem of the documentary sources arises from their

oral beginnings. Because the language of the Britons had no written script, the sole reliance of the people of the island for the sequence of events from the removal of the Roman superstructure to the obliteration of Romano-British society was memory. But they did have certain mnemonic devices, especially the Welsh triad, which sustained recollection by grouping places, events or heroes by threes. They had bards who were official custodians of the folk memory of important happenings, and storytellers who entertained their audiences with more fanciful tales. In the 12th and 13th centuries, parts of the repertories of both kinds of transmitters were written down in the *Four Ancient Books of Wales.*

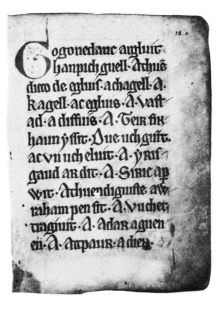

Sporadic references to secular history can likewise be gleaned from writings by or about the saints and theologians of the first flowering of the Celtic church in the 6th and early 7th centuries in Britain and Brittany. A Celtic monk, Gildas, whose life overlapped Arthur's, made an extensive attempt at historical sequence in his *Loss and Conquest of Britain.*

Known as 'the Wise', Gildas became everyone's source. The 8th century English monk, the Venerable Bede, drew on him for the early chapters of his *Ecclesiastical History.* So did another Celtic monk, Nennius, who in the first part of the 9th century compiled the next presentation of secular history in an edition of the *History of the Britons.* He is the first to mention Arthur's name.

In addition to Gildas, Nennius drew on chronicles containing 7th and 8th century data; later editors kept his edition up-to-date, and in the 10th century a year-by-year chronology was appended to it. Still later, it was elaborated by addition of a fanciful list of *Marvels of Britain,* two of which concern Arthur.

17

After the Norman Conquest, in the second quarter of the 12th century, Anglo-Norman writers began to apply themselves to British history. William of Malmesbury wrote his *Acts of the English Kings* and a book *On the Antiquity of the Church of Glastonbury* and Henry of Huntingdon, his *History of the English.*

Then, about 1136, Geoffrey of Monmouth's *History of the Kings of Britain* surrounded rare fact with plentiful fancy and launched the medieval Arthurian legend.

His work was a best-seller—today, more than eight hundred years later, some two hundred manuscript copies survive. Geoffrey's Latin was quickly translated into French, and avidly read alike in France and by the French overlords whom the Conquest had established in England. On the Continent, it supplied story-material for professional litterateurs, whose full-flowered romances used episodes to illustrate the protocol of courtly love with which the French nobility amused itself. Among patrons of the new vogue was Eleanor of Aquitaine, current queen of England as wife of Henry II and former queen of France as wife of Louis VII.

Geoffrey of Monmouth's narrative, however, was not wholly new to Continental ears. During the final phases of the Roman Empire in Britain in the 4th century, and again when Anglo-Saxon pressures were bringing Britain's Dark Age to a close in the 6th, massive emigrations of Britons crossed from Devon and Cornwall to the French peninsula that the Romans had called Armorica and that now became known as Little Britain or Brittany.

Through all the Celtic regions of Britain, and across the water in Celtic Brittany where Merlin was believed to be held in enchanted sleep in the forest of Broceliande, folk names for heights and caves and Stone Age monuments—the megalith known as the *tombeau du roi Arthur* near Paimpont, the *camp d'artus* at Huelgoat, the islet of Aval, the Arthur's Seats, the Arthur's Stones, the Arthur's Ovens, the Arthur's Quoits from Cornwall to Scotland, and the many caves where he and his knights sleep until time to come again—witness the mystique among simple people of the once and future king.

The Ibero-Celts of Brittany were inveterate storytellers. Hard put to it to scratch a living from the meager soil of their rocky land, many wandered eastward in search of livelihood, frequently taking service as mercenaries.

William of Malmesbury derogated "a race . . . . poor at home, and seeking abroad to support a toilsome life by foreign service. Regardless of right and affinity, they decline not even civil war, provided they are paid for it; and, in proportion to remuneration, are ready to enter any service that may be offered." Another commentator declared that "a Kymro (Welshman) has imagination enough for fifty poets without judgment enough for one." But they gave great pleasure to their listeners.

The early 12th century carving on the archivolt of the Porta della Pescheria of the cathedral at Modena in Italy shows Artus de Bretani (Arthur), Galvagnus (Gawain), Che (Kay) and other knights storming a castle where Mardoc (Modred) holds Winlogee (Guenevere) prisoner. It was apparently inspired by Breton stories told in the staging area near Bari where Breton contingents spent the winter of 1096–7 preparing for the First Crusade. At Otranto, in 1167, the Archbishop ordered a mosaic floor for the church; it includes Arthur, crowned and holding a scepter, astride a goat. In front of the goat was a black panther. The derivation is obscure, but the Giant Cat of Lausanne, Capalus, is a reappearance of the Welsh Cath Palug, and Arthur and his knights fight this cat in various Celtic tales.

Breton soldiers were likewise numerous in the army of Norman William; the Conquest enabled many to return to fastnesses in the West Country and Wales abandoned by their forebears four to six centuries before. Geoffrey of Monmouth apparently had Welsh connections.

Transmitted through these various intermediaries, in these various forms, the 'matter of Britain' served a variety of medieval purposes.

Part of its development was a subconscious continuity. In the mountain zone of Britain, from Scotland through Strathclyde and Wales to Devon and Cornwall, lingering pagan memories of gods and heroes, of Druid lore and the Otherworld merged into the mysteries of Merlin and Morgan le Fay, the passing of the king who would come again, the quest of the Grail. The pagan cauldron of plenty was renewed in the Christian chalice. The Celtic version of the withering and burgeoning of the agricultural year fused with the story of the Maimed King. In his ship Prydwen, Arthur visited places of the Otherworld.

But the Arthurian chronicles were likewise used for much more conscious purposes. They were remarkably well suited to adaptation: their sources were remote enough in time and unverifiable enough in content to be malleable no matter how different the ends that the writers who manipulated them had in view.

Geoffrey of Monmouth's version was arranged to serve the dynastic requirements of the Anglo-Norman kings. They needed an independent source for their British sovereignty: as dukes of Normandy they were subject to the heirs of Charlemagne. Jean Bodel's view of the inferiority of all kings to the king of France, written a hundred years after Geoffrey, shows the tenacity of their precedence:

La corone de France doit estre mise avant,
Qar tuit autre roi doivent estre à lui apandant
De la loi crestienne qi an Deu sont creant.

Geoffrey's task was essentially the same as Vergil's in the opening years of the Augustan era, when he created an imperial lineage ascending from Aeneas, vanquisher of King Turnus of Italy and founder of Rome, to Aeneas' father Anchises, Aphrodite's accepted lover, to Anchises' father Priam, king of Troy. Geoffrey's solution came from the same family tree: his British line of kings starts with Aeneas' great-grandson, Brutus, who hears this congenial prophecy from a sibyl:

> Brutus, beyond the setting of the sun, past the realms of Gaul, there lies an island in the sea, once occupied by giants. Now it is empty and ready for your folk. Down the years this will prove an abode suited to you and to your people; and for your descendants it will be a second Troy. A race of kings will be born there from your stock and the round circle of the whole earth will be subject to them.

Thus launched, Geoffrey's genealogy moves rapidly from king to king. Just before reaching Arthur, he introduces a mystical element by inserting his previous work on the *Prophecies of Merlin*. Thereafter, sections of disproportionate length endow Britain with an all-conquering monarch, King Arthur.

Chapter by chapter, Arthur's conquests subject the European continent from Iceland to the Alps; he is on his way to take Rome when messengers recall him to Britain with news of Modred's treachery.

The British kings did not treat this genealogy of their sovereignty as fanciful. In 1141, only five years after its publication, King Stephen relied on it in his contest for the throne with his aunt Matilda. In 1301, Edward I cited it when making his case for dominion over Scotland before Pope Boniface III. In the 15th century, Henry VII

21

advanced it as substantiation of Tudor legitimacy. As late as the 17th century, James I used it in his defense of royal divine right.

A second specific purpose for enlargement of the Arthurian legends animated the monks of Glastonbury when in urgent need of a building fund. In 1184, their wattled church of unknown antiquity was totally destroyed by fire. Their discovery, shortly thereafter, of the graves of Arthur and Guenevere in the monks' cemetery materially increased the revenues from pilgrimages.

Acceptance of Joseph of Arimathea's first century presence in the Isle of Avalon, bearing either the chalice of the Last Supper or two cruets in which he had collected the blood and sweat of the Savior on the Cross, related the Abbey to the mystique of the Grail story and bulwarked the abbot's precedence at oecumenic councils.

The secular authors in France who gave literary form to the Arthurian cycle responded with equal practicality to a sharply contrasting necessity. Their task was to relieve the ennui of castle and court by an escape literature. Under feminine influence, particularly that of Marie of Champagne, Eleanor of Aquitaine's daughter by Louis VII, the establishment of courts of love had supplied the nobility with a new game, prescribing delightfully complicated rules for dainty dalliance between the sexes. A 13th century ivory casket, now

Victoria and Albert Museum. Crown Copyright.

in the Victoria and Albert museum, whose carvings show knights laughingly storming the castle of love while fair ladies on the ramparts pelt them with roses, illustrates the delicate artifice of the new pastime.

Its requirements demanded new characters. Since royal and noble marriages were normally arranged hard-headedly, to strengthen dynasties or families or to unite contiguous lands, romantic love was not expected to flourish between a knight and his wedded lady. The passion, loyalty and devotion extolled in the romances was extra-marital, and the church disapproved in vain. Lancelot, Arthur's perfect knight and his Queen's perfect lover, is a French addition to Arthur's court.

The Round Table of which he became a member was likewise made in France. It is first mentioned in the early 1150's, when Maistre Wace of Caen translated Geoffrey's Latin into French verse as the *Roman de Brut* (these pseudo-histories were called 'Bruts' because they listed Brutus as Britain's first king).

Galahad and the Grail story are introduced a quarter of a century later in Chrétien de Troyes' *Tale of the Grail* and *Perceval,* and Robert de Boron's *Joseph.* De Boron's *Merlin* adds the sword in the stone and the Siege Perilous.

For over a century, the French versions of the cycle sufficed the French-speaking Anglo-Norman society of England. More and more French manuscripts were prepared for and dedicated to noble and royal recipients in England; it was at the English court, between

23

1150–1175, that the French poet Marie de France composed her *Lais*.

But before too long, English and Scottish writers, most of them in the island's peripheral areas, began a process of repatriation, writing in the English vernacular and frequently in the alliterative verse-form that had come into the language with the Anglo-Saxon conquest. The English works were for the most part translations of French originals, but in their settings they brought Arthur home again.

The final repatriation, this time of the entire cycle, came at the end of the 15th century, as the medieval period closed. In 1485, William Caxton published Sir Thomas Malory's monumental translation, the *Morte Darthur,* as one of England's earliest printed books.

During the Renaissance and the Enlightenment, writers largely ignored the Arthurian material. Holinshed's *Chronicles of England, Scotland and Ireland* are replete with accounts of his activities, and the

24

centenary edition of Malory came out between the first and second editions of Holinshed. But while Shakespeare as well as the other Elizabethan dramatists mined Holinshed, he chose his early kings from pre-Roman times—Cymbeline, Lear—and his later ones from the Anglo-Norman Henrys and Richard.

Milton very nearly made the Arthurian theme the basis of his major work; the hesitation that preceded his decision to use Biblical material instead can be documented from his carefully annotated copy of Gildas and from notes written in 1639–40 projecting a history of Britain from the landing of Brutus to the time of King Arthur: "I will someday recall in song the things of my native land, and Arthur who carried war even into fairy land. Or I shall tell of those great-hearted champions bound in the society of the Round Table, and (O may the spirit be in me!) I shall break the Saxon phalanx with British war."

The determining factor in turning him away from the subject was probably the claim to Arthurian ancestry advanced by the Stuarts of whom he disapproved: in the epic he finally wrote he announced himself glad not

> . . . to dissect
> With long and tedious havoc fabl'd knights
> In Battles feigned.

Then in the 19th century, Arthur of Britain came into extensive vogue again.

Through these amazingly diverse presentations of his story, over the better part of a thousand years, Arthur the Dark Age hero left his name on the British land. The local habitations of his legend range from stones, heights and caves to the Iron Age fort at South Cadbury in Somerset, long known as Camelot, to Glastonbury Abbey, to the Round Table in Winchester Castle on which the seats of the companions are indicated radiating from a Tudor rose.

Because the realms of Arthur are so many and so diverse, I have described my explorations by major periods and by main types of literary text.

25

My two initial ventures are to realms of solid, if sparse history. The first is a tour of the Romano-British society that remaining British leaders attempted to defend after the Romans were gone. The plans and resources of these leaders stemmed from Roman policies and capabilities developed while the legions were still there; their basis for common action was the tribal structure which the Romans had found when they came and through which they established local government.

The next expedition seeks the places where these last Romano-British kings and their commanders may have lived and fought, and hazards a guess that Arthur's charisma dates from a major military victory following which, for half a century, the incoming Saxon tide reversed and ebbed.

Thereafter, sources become more literary. The Welsh bardic tradition is first among major expressions of the 'matter of Britain'; its tantalizing absence of sequence and jaw-breaking plethora of proper names nevertheless convey a good measure of underlying fact; some of the persons and places it identifies are indisputably authentic. The places mentioned by Geoffrey of Monmouth localize many of the most attractive surviving fictions in some of the most spectacular Arthurian shrines.

In their geography, the "Frensshe bookes" and other Continental romances that next took up the tale incline toward the vagueness of geographic unfamiliarity: the author of the 13th century *Garel von dem Bluehenden Tal,* writing in Salzburg, combines British and Breton landscape in describing Arthur's Whitsun feast as held at Dinazrun (Dinas Bran in Wales) at the edge of the forest of Priziljan (Broceliande in Brittany).

Mostly, the place-names used in other contexts as scenes of Arthur's crowning, courts and tournaments are of centers that were either well-known abroad, like Britain's successive Saxon and Norman capitals at Winchester and London, or that had been made memorable by recent history—Henry V sailed from Southampton, why not Arthur?
Moreover, most of the fantasies of these accounts could be located only in Never-Never land.

The Glastonbury fables, by strict contrast, have their local habitation in a landscape where readily identifiable background is available for each detail.

Similarly, the directly observed descriptions of nature and the English countryside that freshen the pages of medieval English translators from the French invite expeditions into literary geography.

The milepost zero of the explorations reported in these chapters should be the British Museum. My hours of concentrated enjoyment of manuscripts and early books were there, although other great libraries, from Cambridge to Aberystwyth in Great Britain, and from the Bibliothèque Nationale in Paris to the Morgan collection in New York, have contributed to my illustrations.

The other indispensable source of documentation was the Ordnance Survey's special maps of Roman and Dark Age Britain and inch-to-the-mile grids of contemporary roads. With these, plus the companionable sixth sense of Francis Pickens Miller to anticipate a contour in advance of its coming into view, even a spot by all the world forgot could be located.

The mileage necessary to cover the range of a military mobile force bent on holding nearly as much of Britain as the Romans ever held is surprising. And when to this mileage is added a tour of the Roman installations from which the Romano-Britons took their strategy, visits to the sites where Celtic myths placed Arthur's name and where medieval legend located his birthplace and his courts, some

27

of his knights' adventures, and the last battle that preceded either his passing or his burial, the total is more surprising still. A figure of 5,000 miles is not extravagant. But a completed overview of these places is as rewarding as a series of successful fast deployments must have been to the historic Arthur, or an honorable outcome to a sequence of episodes in a perilous quest would have seemed to a knight of the legendary king.

To the historians and archaeologists working on the Dark Age period and the scholars of Arthurian literature and heraldry who gave me both advice and insights, the thanks of this itinerant journalist are offered. The mistakes in the record are mine.

THE
ROMANO–
BRITISH
SOCIETY

From the beginning, the story of Britain was part of the story of the Continent. Powerful waves of prehistoric arrival, originating far eastward, flung themselves across the Channel to spread over Europe's western island. The Normans were the last successful invaders, but their predecessors were many; William the Conqueror crossed from lands previously occupied in northwest France, but other northerners—Saxon, Jute, Frisian, Angle, Dane—came directly, earlier, and before their time Britain was a Roman province for an era as long as from Queen Elizabeth I to the present day.

Caesar undertook an invasion because the tribes that gave him trouble in Gaul had settlements in England. The tribal structure that preceded his arrival was tamed and systematized, but also encouraged and developed under Roman administration; it was what survived the Roman overlay. Britain's Dark Age leaders were the products of this society; the imperial structure determined the extent and the limitations of British preparation for independent responsibility. Their

30

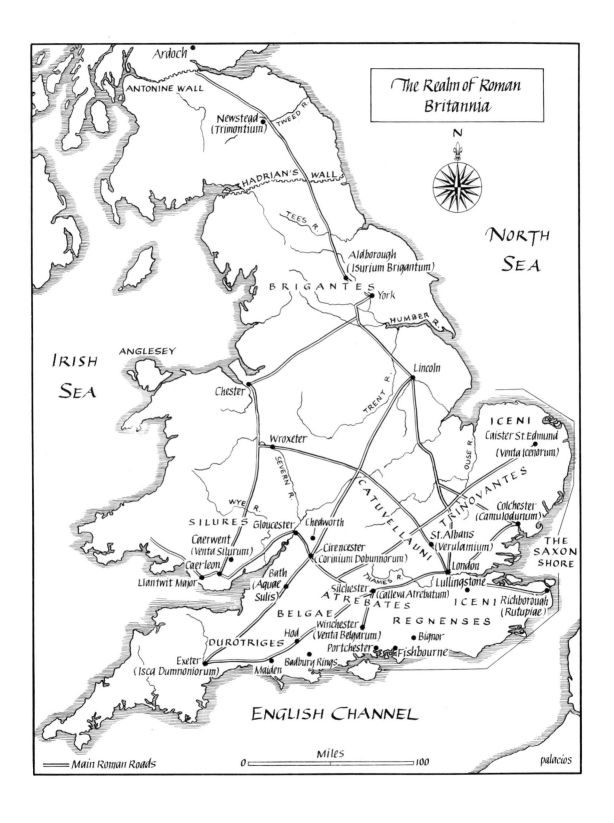

The Realm of Roman Britannia

N

Ardoch

ANTONINE WALL

Newstead
(Trimontium)

TWEED R.

HADRIAN'S WALL

TEES R.

NORTH
SEA

Aldborough
(Isurium Brigantum)

B R I G A N T E S

York

HUMBER R.

IRISH
SEA

ANGLESEY

Lincoln

I C E N I

Caister St. Edmund
(Venta Icenorum)

Chester

TRENT R.

OUSE R.

Wroxeter

SEVERN R.

C A T U V E L L A U N I

T R I N O V A N T E S

Colchester
(Camulodunum)

WYE R.

S I L U R E S   Gloucester   Chedworth

Caerwent
(Venta Silurum)

Caer-leon

Llantwit Major

Cirencester
(Corinium Dobunnorum)

St. Albans
(Verulamium)

London

THE
SAXON
SHORE

Bath
(Aquae
Sulis)

Silchester
(Calleva Atrebatum)

THAMES R.

Lullingstone

A T R E B A T E S

I C E N I   Richborough
(Rutupiae)

B E L G A E

Winchester
(Venta Belgarum)

R E G N E S E S

DUROTRIGES

Hod

Bignor

Portchester

Fishbourne

Exeter
(Isca Dumnoniorum)

Maiden

Badbury Rings

ENGLISH CHANNEL

Miles

Main Roman Roads   0   100   palacios

way of life in the 5th and early 6th centuries, and their defense strategy, derived from the Roman years.

allia," Caesar observed in his *Commentaries,* "est omnis divisa in partes tres." But he found there was a fourth part as well. British tribesmen made Roman successes in Gaul provisional and temporary by supplying their Gallic cousins with reinforcements for military victory and refuges for withdrawal and redeployment in moments of defeat. Caesar observed that

> The interior of Britain is inhabited by people who claim, on the strength of an oral tradition, to be aboriginal; the coast, by Belgic immigrants who came to plunder and make war—nearly all of them retaining the names of the tribes from which they originated—and later settled down to till the soil. The population is exceedingly large, the ground thickly studded with homesteads, closely resembling those of the Gauls, and the cattle very numerous. . . . By far the most civilized inhabitants are those living in Kent (a purely maritime district) whose way of life differs little from that of the Gauls. Most of the tribes in the interior do not grow corn but live on milk and meat and wear skins. All the Britons dye their bodies with woad, which produces a blue color, and this gives them a more terrifying appearance in battle. They wear their hair long, and shave the whole of their bodies except the head and upper lip.

> [In 55 B.C.] Caesar made active preparations for an expedition to Britain, because he knew that in almost all the Gallic camps the Gauls had received reinforcements from the Britons, Caesar sent Commius whom he had made king of the Atrebates after the conquest of that tribe and who was greatly respected in Britain to urge as many tribes as possible to submit.

32   Though his official account of this first invasion was sufficiently glowing to induce a twenty-day public thanksgiving in Rome, his

effort was only marginally successful: during his crossing, Channel currents and the high Atlantic tides of a full moon disabled many ships, and the unaccustomed necessity of disembarking, fully armed and under attack, in deep water,

> frightened our soldiers . . . . with the result that they did not show the same alacrity and enthusiasm as they usually did in battles on dry land.

After two engagements, having garnered some hostages, Caesar withdrew. Next year, he did better. He fought at the Medway and at the ford of the Thames between Chelsea and Battersea, where the Celtic shield in the British Museum was retrieved in our time. His engineers joined the gravel banks on opposite sides of the river at Westminster with London's first bridge.

33

Caesar's native ally and legate, Commius, was intermediary when Cassivelaunus, the Catuvellauni's tribal leader, surrendered; the terms included payment of annual tribute. Other tribes, among them the Trinovantes who lived northeast of London, voluntarily sent peacemaking envoys. Caesar departed well pleased.

Two years later, Commius pleased him considerably less: he joined Vercingetorix in the widespread revolt of 52 B.C. in Gaul, and when Caesar put it down escaped with impunity to found a kingdom of British Atrebates that extended from the Isle of Wight to the Thames Valley.

Thereafter, for close to a century, the British tribes, untroubled by invasion, devoted themselves to inter-tribal war: in the 20's B.C. the king of the Catuvellauni conquered the tribes in the south and east and negotiated payment of Caesar's tribute into customs duties. His son—Shakespeare's Cymbeline—absorbed the Trinovantes and from a new capital at Camulodunum (Colchester) ruled Britain from Derbyshire to Somerset.

British wealth increased: the historian Strabo names wheat, cattle, gold, silver, iron, hides, slaves and hunting dogs as the island's chief exports; later, Juvenal praised its oysters. In exchange, British chieftains acquired glass and pottery from factories in Gaul and Italy, Mediterranean wine in graceful amphorae, and such luxuries as tableware, bronze-plated furniture and adornments of amber or ivory. The second Roman invasion was directed toward control of resources as much as pacification.

In 43 A.D., four legions, the II Augusta, the IX Hispana, the XIV Gemina and the XX Valeria Victrix initiated the permanent occupation of Britain. When success was assured, the Emperor Claudius arrived in person. The landing was again in the southeast, this time at Rutupiae (Richborough) in Kent. There, a permanent fortress was erected; its massive walls and the cruciform base of a monument to the success of the invasion endure today. The walls of the monument were shortly encased in Carrara marble. It expressed the new power in the land.

THE REALMS OF ARTHUR

Battle was joined at London Bridge; thereafter, the flat lands of the eastern parts of the island offered few obstacles. A Roman walled city rapidly took shape at Camulodunum (Colchester), then renamed Colonia Claudia Victricensis and centered on a temple to the state religion with fifty foot columns and a cult statue of Claudius of which the head is now in the British Museum. A second city rose at Verulamium (St. Albans). Further north, a legionary fortress was built at Lindum (Lincoln), followed by another at Eboracum (York).

Control of these areas was essential to the Romans' pacification policy; to tap the island's mineral resources, troops had to move west.

They started from a staging point of assured loyalty: in southeastern England, with its capital at Noviomagus (Chichester) was the kingdom of the Regnenses, a tribe which enjoyed a very special relationship with Rome. Its name came from 'regnum'—a kingdom, and its ruler during the last quarter of the first century held the unique title of *rex et legatus Augusti in Britannia;* Tiberius Claudius Cogidubnus was at one and the same time a native king and a Roman official.

His status has been known since 1723, when an inscribed stone was found in Chichester attesting the dedication of a temple by the local guild of metal workers to Neptune, god of the sea by which their ore reached them from mines in the Weald, and Minerva, patron of craftsmen, and also, by express order of the ruler, to the Roman god-emperor, pro salute domus divinae.

But in the 1960's, a chance discovery has revealed the sumptuous, Roman-style surroundings in which he lived, at Fishbourne just west of Chichester. Lying close to what at that period was the shore-line of the sea, a hundred-room palace begun about 70 A.D. and enclosing some 250,000 square feet has now been about half excavated; part of it was opened as a museum in 1968. The colonnades of its four five-hundred foot wings surrounded a formal garden resembling the more extensive gardens of Rome and like them adorned with fountains (conduit pipes and the cistern supplying them have been unearthed), planted with ornamental trees (cypress, flowering cherry), and gay with flower-beds beside broad box-bordered walkways. Guest suites had private verandahs and dining rooms; the great audience chamber was raised above the level of the rest of the palace. Numerous mosaic floors, the earlier ones with geometric designs and the later with elaborate patterns, have been uncovered in an exceptionally fine state of preservation. Door cornices were of marble; stone used included not only English Purbeck but varieties from the Pyrenees, Carrara, Greece and Asia Minor. The palace entrance and the king's personal apartments, still covered by modern buildings, await exploration.

But beyond Cogidubnus' territories the legions met resistance; once across the downs, on entering hilly country, they encountered defense structures which the tribes had used long before their time, and used again against the Saxons after their departure. As the II Augusta, led by the future emperor Vespasian, fought its way across Dorset, Wiltshire and Somerset, the British mounted resistance at more than twenty of the hill forts that Suetonius calls 'oppida.' Caesar had said, "The Britons apply the term 'strongholds' to densely wooded spots fortified with a rampart and trench, to which they retire in order to escape the attacks of invaders;" the hill forts of the south and west were more formidable but similar.

Two millennia earlier, with picks made from the antlers of the red deer, Stone Age peoples had shaped causewayed enclosures for autumn round-ups and culling of herds; Iron Age men entrenched them further; British tribesmen topped them with palisades sheathed with stone. Forts that the Romans stormed (too many of them today confusingly known as 'castles') almost certainly included Badbury Rings and Spettisbury Rings southeast of Blandford Forum, and Maiden below Dorchester in Dorset. Maiden (the name comes from 'dunum'—stronghold), ringed by four concentric circles of immense ditches, enclosed an area as large as a legionary fortress. Its ramparts

still silhouette the sky, and the foundations of a late Roman temple are in its precincts. Two other major hill-forts, Hambledon Hill and Hod Hill, stand northwest of Blandford Forum; the Romans converted Hod into a fortress from which to exercise surveillance over Wessex.

In approaching these forts, the Romans held their long, semi-cylindrical shields above their heads in a close formation known as the testudo (turtle); while they climbed under this cover their archers rained arrows on the stone-throwing defenders above. Skeletons at excavated cemeteries give witness of their fighting methods: a rib-cage pierced by an arrow-tip, a skull perforated by a throwing-spear, a spinal column with an iron-sheathed ballistic bolt wedged between the discs.

As they pressed on west, the Romans set an initial frontier on a line running from Glevum (Gloucester) to Viroconium Cornoviarum (Wroxeter), but converted the latter into a supply center after they sealed off the restless Welsh peninsula by major fortresses at Isca Silurum (Caerleon) on the River Usk above the Severn Estuary and

40

Deva (Chester) east of the Wirral on the River Dee. Isca Dumnoniorum (Exeter) kept similar watch over the Devon-Cornwall peninsula. In the area enclosed by these defense-lines, a Romanized society developed and became the Romano-Britons' heritage.

Prior to the conquest, tribal transport had been by water or by immemorial footpaths along the crest of high land: the Icknield Way can still be walked from Salisbury Plain over most of the miles to Brancaster in Norfolk. Thereafter, the chief Roman installations were connected by a system of arrow-straight, admirably surveyed and meticulously surfaced roads, raised on causeways above marshy ground and bridged at rivers.

Considerable parts of this system became a boon not only to the Romano-Britons, but to modern traffic as well. The *Antonine Itinerary*, 41 an early 3rd century road guide to the entire empire, shows sixteen main roads radiating from London to fortresses and tribal capitals, but today's traveller, whether in Britain, on the Continent, or in the East, when he tops a contour with the way straight and clear before him, mile after mile, needs no book to tell him by whom the foundations of his route were laid.

In 78 A.D., the northward military advance was resumed with the arrival of Agricola, the general who carried the Roman standards into Scotland to Ardoch and Inchtuthill and outposts still further above Perth. Part way up, he set the fort of Trimontium (Newstead) near the Eildon Hills on the south bank of the Tweed, where excavations show that further fighting took place in Arthur's time.

Down the centuries, this northern frontier was never stable for long. Tacitus, reporting on Agricola's campaigns, puts in the mouth of a Caledonian chief the hatred felt by the frontier tribes and witnessed a few years earlier in the savagery of Boudicca's revolt:

Today the uttermost parts of Britain are laid bare; there are no other tribes to come; nothing but sea and cliffs and these more deadly Romans, whose arrogance you shun in vain by obedience and self-restraint. Harriers of the world, now that earth fails their all-devastating hands, they probe even the sea: if their enemy have wealth, they have greed; if he be poor, they are ambitious; East nor West has glutted them; alone of all mankind they behold with the same passion of concupiscence waste alike and want. To plunder, butcher, steal, these things they misname empire: they make a desolation and they call it peace.

Children and kin are by the law of nature each man's dearest possessions; they are swept away from us by conscription to be slaves in other lands: our wives and sisters, even when they escape a soldier's lust, are debauched by self-styled friends and guests: our goods and chattels go for tribute; our lands and harvests in requisitions of grain; life and limb themselves are used up in levelling marsh and forest to the accompaniment of gibes and blows. Slaves born to slavery are sold once for all and are fed by their masters free of cost; but Britain pays a daily price for her own enslavement, and feeds the slavers. . . . .

Bitterness such as this forced repeated shifts in the Romans' northern strategy: the lines that commanders tried to hold frequently had enemies on both sides. The Brigantes' territory crossed the entire island above York, and in 119 they rose. Details of the massacre are unknown, but it wiped one of the four legions on the island, the IX Hispana, from the pages of history.

Next year, inspecting the island in person, the Emperor Hadrian ordered built the wall that bears his name. In remarkable completeness, its course still runs from the Solway Estuary west of Carlisle to the Tyne's approach to the North Sea at Wall's End. Seventy-three miles long, with milecastles at every mile, turrets between the milecastles, and a supply depot to the rear at Corstopitum (Corbridge), the structure's seventeen main forts quartered complete units of infantry or cavalry, with HQ, commander's house, barracks and baths, hospitals, latrines, stables, granaries.

Yet this monumental barrier, though some of its forts were periodically re-used—perhaps in Arthur's time as well—was fully maintained for only sixteen years; in 138, the Emperor Antoninus Pius ordered the frontier pushed north, and a turf wall built across the thirty-eight miles of the island's narrowest waist, from Bridgeness on the Firth of Forth to Old Kilpatrick on the Firth of Clyde.

Caledonian incursions very shortly overran this defense; later they, the Picts and the Scots united to break Hadrian's Wall as well,

and in 211 Caracalla abandoned all territory north of it. Because of these troubles, the Romans were inclined to welcome as buffer-zone allies rather than repel as invaders the Anglian and Frisian settlers who arrived in the latter centuries of the occupation and were allowed to establish themselves in northeastern England.

Like the Picts and the Caledonians, the Iberians and Celts of western Wales and the Devon-Cornwall peninsula beyond Exeter remained on the fringes of empire. The Romans worked copper and lead mines in these areas, as well as the gold mines at Dolaucothi in Carmarthenshire which served the Romans then and provide ore for the wedding rings of British royalty now—the National Museum at Cardiff displays the water-wheels by which lodes were kept drained.

But these were government operations with slave labor; Roman villas in the region are scarce. The other Roman installations were forts and fortlets to safeguard transportation of the ore by land or sea.

In the society that shaped up behind the military lines, Roman law, language and customs overlaid British tribal society. The resulting way of life lasted as long as the empire. After Rome crumbled, it was likewise the way of life that the Romano-Britons of Arthur's time attemped to defend against the next invasion, as Anglo-Saxon long-boats landed a new population on British shores.

Examination of the range of activities open to Romano-Britons while Rome was in control, and of the areas of public life from which they were barred, shows the extent to which the men who took over when Rome was gone had received previous training and experience, and the extent to which those 5th century British leaders and their military commanders suddenly found themselves performing functions hitherto unfamiliar.

Two major functions were strictly reserved by the Roman occupiers for their exclusive exercise: governmental relations between the province of Britain and the central authorities at Rome, and all aspects of military activity.

Until the empire was in decline, no political representation of the island as a whole was permitted to indigenous leadership. Indigenous military skills developed among the British tribes on the borders of Roman control, and during occasional uprisings within the Roman lines, but the legions were imperial. It is probable that the Romano-British political leaders of the 5th century acquired some of their military strength by persuading peripheral commanders to make common cause with them against the new invasion—indeed, whether Arthur was a Romano-Briton or a British tribal captain is still unknown.

The way of life of the Roman legions, lived by the book across the entire empire, made no provision for a local habitation anywhere. The very fort-plans exhibit the completeness of the army's existence entirely separate from the life of whatever country a legionary might

have as his station at any given time. Even a temporary marching-camp set up at the end of the day by troops on the move was laid out according to rule: as soon as lines of known length had been staked out, every soldier knew where each facility from HQ to cook-house was to go, and his part in putting it there.

In the course of his 22-year term of service he expected to traverse many lands; the climate and fighting qualities of the local population might differ, but his day-to-day routine did not. Fraternization with camp-followers excepted, to live under the eagles was to live apart.

Steles found in Britain of legionaries who died in service there show how far many travelled from enlistment to grave; the body of Barates of Palmyra in the Syrian desert was laid to rest at Chesters on the Wall; in the Shrewsbury Museum, "Gaius Mannius Secundus, son of Gaius, of the tribe Pollias, Born at Pollentia, soldier of the XX Legion, 52 years old. 31 years of service, attached as orderly to the Governor of the Province, lies here."

47

The units of lightly-armed auxiliary troops, called alae, that supplemented legionary strength, though recruited in the provinces, were never stationed in their own countries: British auxiliaries were in service by Agricola's time, but in the Province of Pannonia on the Danube, not Britannia.

A legionary might draw closer to a local community when his term expired; the army maintained coloniae for old soldiers at Colchester, Lincoln, York and Gloucester, and here a veteran might settle down and transmit the rudiments of military procedure to attentive local boys. But during his active service the Romano-Britons and he lived apart.

The exclusiveness of the Roman military structure was paralleled in civilian matters by the sole charge exercised by the Governor General over relations with Rome. Fiscal and legal authority was similarly vested in an imperial civil service, and Roman civilians managed the mines and other enterprises operated with slave labor on behalf of the government. In addition, Roman traders visited the island, and some of the agricultural villas were owned and occupied by families from Italy.

But at subordinate levels of government, Romano-British civilians found, and were encouraged to find, scope for their political and administrative abilities. Throughout the empire, self-administration according to local custom was the rule: it was Roman policy to devolve local government on subject peoples. Under Caracalla, Roman citizenship was extended to freemen in all provinces. A Romano-British upper class developed, supported by agriculture or trade and served by slaves, whether in the tribal capitals shown on the map on page 31 or in country villas. Tacitus' *Agricola* analyzes Roman motives for encouraging adoption of this way of life:

In order that a population scattered and uncivilized, and proportionately ready for war, might be habituated by comfort to peace and quiet, he (Agricola) would exhort individuals, assist communities, to erect temples, market-places, houses: he praised the energetic, rebuked the indolent, and the rivalry for his compliments took the place of coercion. Moreover he began to train the sons of the chieftains in a liberal education, and to give preference to the native talents of the Briton as against the plodding Gaul. As a result, the nation which used to reject the Latin language began to aspire to rhetoric; further, the wearing of our dress became a distinction, and the toga came into fashion, and little by little the Britons were seduced into alluring vices: to the lounge, the bath, the well-appointed dinner table. The simple natives gave the name of 'culture' to this factor of their slavery.

Yet for over three hundred years, the social pattern thus established proved workable.

Among the tribal capitals where Romano-British men of substance exercised the functions of local government, Silchester has been thoroughly excavated; its city plan shows that their surroundings included a town hall, temples, market area, shops, baths very similar to those of a Mediterranean Roman city. The site has been covered up again for agricultural use, but a scale model of the town and most of the smaller finds are in the Reading Museum.

Among the latter is a bronze horse very similar in style to the White Horse carved into the chalk of the downs at Uffington in Berkshire in the 1st century A.D. and the horses on the pre-conquest gold coins of various southeastern tribes. It is shown on page 67.

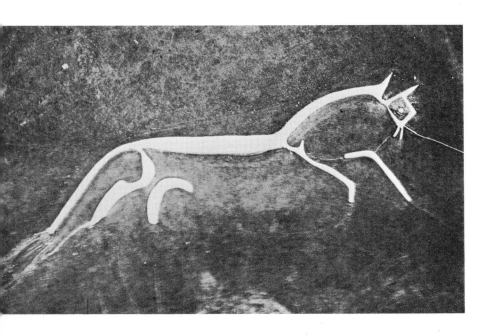

Likewise in the museum is a cast (the original is privately held) of a bronze eagle, possibly part of the decoration of Silchester's city hall, but also possibly from the top of a legionary standard. The slots where its outspread wings were once inserted are empty now; there is a look of outrage in its eye.

Other tribal capitals have been at least partially explored. At Aldborough, a number of well-preserved mosaics have been uncovered, and part of the town wall, which illustrates the art of political compromise by exhibiting the stone facing favored by the Romans on one side and the turfed bevel preferred by the Brigantes on the other. At Caerwent, the riverside capital of the Silures near Caerleon, foundations of numerous houses have been cleared and walls and watchtowers stand high.

The Romano-British tribal towns, and cities such as Colchester and St. Albans where later building has not encroached on early sites, all exhibit similar plans: a center for government and trade, surrounding residential streets, sometimes an amphitheater or odeon, and a variety of provision for religious observances.

The state religion was typified by the temple at Colchester. The council of representatives of all of the tribes formed in connection with this worship was in early years a ceremonial body, but at the end of the empire its sessions appear to have afforded a means of concerting a unified policy for political cooperation after the Roman withdrawal.

Normally, the empire was tolerant of local cults, but soon after the invasion, military action to stamp out one set of religious practices

51

took Roman troops all the way to the Isle of Anglesey on the Welsh shore of the Irish Sea. Probably rightly, the Romans suspected the Druids of ritual human sacrifice, and in any case held their priests' exercise of political as well as religious authority to constitute a secular threat.

Caesar notes that these dignitaries, exempt from taxes and military service, served as judges in disputes ranging from boundaries to murder, and that

> any individual or tribe failing to accept their award is banned from taking part in sacrifice. . . . On a fixed date in each year they hold a session in a consecrated spot in the country of the Carnutes, which is supposed to be the center of Gaul. . . . The Druidic doctrine is believed to have been found existing in Britain and thence imported into Gaul; even today those who want to make a profound study of it generally go to Britain for the purpose.

Tacitus describes the eerie engagement that destroyed the Druid holy of holies, root and branch:

> On the beach stood the adverse array, a serried mass of arms and men, with women flitting between the ranks. In the style of the Furies, in robes of deathly black and with dishevelled hair, they brandished their torches; while a circle of Druids lifting their hands to heaven and showering imprecations, struck the troops with such awe at the extraordinary spectacle that, as though their limbs were paralyzed, they exposed their bodies to wounds without an attempt at movement. Then, reassured by their general, and inciting each other never to flinch before a band of females and fanatics, they charged behind their standards, cut down all who met them, and enveloped the enemy in his own flames. The next step was to install a garrison among the conquered population, and to demolish the groves consecrated to their savage cults; for they consider it a pious duty to slake the altars with captive blood and to consult their deities by means of human entrails.

52

Among Roman soldiers, the eastern god Mithras was a favorite:

various shrines to him have been found at military installations, and one was revealed in the heart of the City of London by the World War II blitz. The goddess Sul Minerva presided at Aquae Sulis (Bath)—the bearded Gorgon's head from her temple pediment is unique in Romano-British art. The temple to Nodens, inaccessible in a private park near Lydney in Gloucestershire, instances adoption of the Celtic god Nuada. Nuada was king of the gods who came to Ireland from Norway and nothern Scotland and conquered the aborigines; in the initial engagement he lost an arm, but was fitted with a jointed silver hand by Dian Cécht the physician; the Lydney site is arranged rather like an asclepeion, with a dormitory, a hospital and baths as well as a sanctuary.

Archaeological opinion is swinging in favor of designating a major building at Silchester as an early Christian church. According to various chronicles, the British were Christianized soon: in 167 one Lucius, king of Britain, is said to have sent letters to Pope Eleutherius asking that he and his people be taken into the church; the pope "carried out what he asked." Both before and after Constantine adopted Christianity as the empire's official religion, however, British Christianity traversed the same rocky road that lay before it else-where: persecutions made martyrs of St. Alban, St. Julian, St. Aaron and St. Julius of Caerleon, and London's Bishop Angulus.

53

The Romano-Britons who lived according to Mediterranean patterns in the tribal capitals had counterparts in the country gentlemen who lived in villas in the areas suited to agriculture.

Avoiding the marshes that bordered many rivers and the practically impenetrable primeval forest that crossed the island from York and Lincoln to the Severn, such farms clustered on the flat lands of Kent and East Anglia, the grassy edges of the downs and the lightly forested uplands of Sussex, Hampshire and Wiltshire, the higher land east of the Severn Estuary around Bath and the rim of the Glastonbury marshes from Yeovil to Taunton.

Their owners modified the villa architecture of Italy with certain concessions to the British climate: where the Roman villa grouped its principal rooms around a central court or atrium British plans usually placed a row of rooms along a south-facing colonnade. Additions formed an L or a U at its ends; agricultural outbuildings stood nearby.

The more pretentious British villas offered all the amenities, however, from hypocausts for central heating to elaborate baths, familiar in upper-class Rome; dining-room floor plans were designed so that the triclinium disposed three diners' couches around an apse open-ended for service on the fourth side. Principal rooms were

floored with mosaics made by British workmen from standard patterns prepared in Rome: the Vatican Museum still contains the elaborate design showing the story of Aeneas that floored a British villa at Low Ham near Montacute in Devon, now shown in the Taunton Museum.

Some of the mosaics indicate Christian ownership, with a chi rho, an alpha and omega, or the figure of a saint. The large villa

55

at Lullingstone near Eynsford in Kent, occupied for over three hundred years, bespeaks both pagan and Christian worship. In one of its upper-level rooms, a Christian chapel during the latter years of the villa's use and a Christian church thereafter, elaborate wall-paintings showed elegantly dressed personages in an attitude of supplication. Yet below stairs, contemporary with the chapel, in front of marble portrait busts now in the British Museum, votive pots served pagan rituals. A new owner remodelled this villa in the first third of the 4th century; he installed central heating, elaborate mosaic floors of which the dining-room design is almost intact, and blue-green window-glass.

Some of the later inhabitants of the villa at Chedworth near Northleach in Gloucestershire were likewise Christians; at Bignor near Chichester, on the contrary, the mosaics show only Roman gods and goddesses—Venus looks on while cupids battle gladiators; Zeus in the form of an eagle carries away Ganymede.

The richness of villa furnishings is periodically recalled by discoveries of hoards buried in the years of growing danger of attack and never recovered by their owners. In 1735, a blacksmith's daughter gathering firewood on the banks of the Tyne came upon a 4th century silver dish, nineteen inches across and decorated with mythological scenes. The silver plate of the Mildenhall treasure, exhibited in the British Museum, was chanced on by a ploughman in 1942; its magnificent condition is in sharp contrast to that of a similar find at Traprain Law in Scotland, where a quantity of repoussé silver had apparently been deliberately flattened by thieves eager to make a compact cache.

Villa pottery included both imports and domestic manufactures. Mediterranean wine arrived in amphorae; factories in Gaul provided red 'Samian' ware in quantity, and fine pieces from Cologne are represented by the 4th century glass bowl found at Wint Hill in Somerset

57

and now in Oxford's Ashmolean Museum; it is engraved with a hunt scene around which inscribed Latin and Greek phrases wish the drinker good health. Celtic potters within the island contributed a distinctive ornamentation; their designs show gracefully flowing lines or figures of running dogs or deer. The museums of Colchester and Verulamium exhibit superb examples of their work, including the 'Colchester Vase' with sparring gladiators.

Such was the standard of living to which upper-class Romano-Britons became accustomed. The families who grew up in this culture, the citizens of substance who set the tone of tribal life, can be in-

stanced by the landed proprietor Calpurnius whose son Patrick, born about 389, became the patron saint of Ireland. The father was a decurion and a deacon whose place, Bannauenta, is thought to have been in the Severn area, perhaps in Glamorganshire; his father before him is known to have been a presbyter.

Toward the end of the 4th century, massive abandonment of villa sites plainly evidences the growth of insecurity and fear, though no single indication on a farm is as poignant as the man's skeleton, found wedged between the pillars of a hypocaust of the public baths at Wroxeter where he had crawled, a hoard of coins in hand. Yet limited occupation of parts of villas persisted for some generations; in southwest Wales, the family that produced the 6th century saint, Illtud, continued to live the life of country gentlemen, though after the good days were gone with the wind they moved from their house to their barn. That was where the saint founded the monastery of Llantwit Major, and trained such renowned monks as Gildas, author of the *Loss and Conquest of Britain*.

60

Curiously enough, though the lands the Saxons first occupied in the southeast were the richest part of the arable zone, the invaders avoided the former villas. Charring on mosaic floors—it can be seen in the Verulamium museum and at Lullingstone—shows that some-one used them as hearths during the decline, but no Saxon dwelling has been found on top of a Romano-British site.

By the close of the 4th century, the Roman imperial structure was being torn apart. Of the hundred emperors who ruled between 46 B.C. and 457 A.D. only forty-one died natural deaths; the scramble for power intensified as central authority crumbled. More and more responsibility had to be exercised locally; legions on the frontiers began to proclaim as emperors favorite leaders under whom they

served. The earliest of these, Diocletian, was named by troops on the Bosphorus in 284; he and his colleague Maximianus were the first emperors not to reside in Rome.

The idea caught on in the West. After Saxon long-boats were reported in the Channel in 282, the Romans detailed a patrol fleet under a commander with a new title, Comes litoris Saxonici, the Count of the Saxon Shore. In 286 one Carausius obtained this command, and on the strength of his naval power set himself up as emperor. Diocletian and Maximianus shortly accepted him as Augustus of Britain.

Like theirs, however, his tenure was brief and terminated by violence; one of his subordinates, Allectus, murdered and supplanted him in 293. Three years later, the then Caesar of the West, Constantius Chlorus, reconquered Gaul, crossed the Channel, and eliminated Allectus.

This episode left a special legacy to Britain's subsequent defenders. In Carausius' time, the Channel coasts were ringed with a powerful series of walled fortifications. Old strongholds like Rutupiae were strengthened, and a number of new ones built on the south coast. Later, these were known as the Forts of the Saxon Shore. But some of the new structures,—Anderida (Pevensey) and Portus Adurni (Portchester) seem too imposing and too early to have been induced by Saxon appearances that for some decades remained a minor threat. A guess is that Carausius may have looked toward Rome and anticipated, quite correctly, that usurpation was unlikely to continue undisturbed. The daily seep-seep of encroaching tides has leached some of these installations away. but at Portchester the entire circuit of walls and gates stands barely diminished. In the Dark Age, Arthur is believed to have led a hard-fought and losing battle against the Saxons here.

MAXIMIANUS

CARAUSIUS

ALLECTUS

CONSTANTIUS CHLORUS

During the 4th and early 5th century, as the tempo of barbarian attack quickened in all parts of the empire, local Roman continuity in the maintenance of order was increasingly replaced by temporary military aid sent in at critical moments under a special commander, or by self-help under a usurper. Increasingly, too, troop withdrawals drained fighting power from Britain.

In 368, after the Irish, Picts, Saxons, Atecotti and Franks, in concert, from the west, north and east, had attacked and overwhelmed the Dux Britanniarum and the Comes litoris Saxonici, Theodosius the Elder was dispatched as Governor General of Britain. He restored order, then departed for other tasks.

In 383, a new thrust of Picts was countered by a usurper, Magnus Clemens Maximus, a Spaniard who had made his career as a commander in Britain. Proclaimed emperor by the legions there, he shortly invaded the Continent, taking with him substantial forces. When Theodosius defeated him in Italy, these troops were permanently lost to Britain. (Theodosius memorialized the defeat in Constantinople, where an inscription on the central arch of his Golden Gate still announces that it was built "post fata tyranni"—after the downfall of the usurper.)

In the 390's, the Irish overran Wales. Stilicho, Magister Militum of the West, arrived and retrieved the territory, then hastened back to block new barbaric thrusts into Italy. As the stream of Visigothic and Teutonic invaders continued, he recalled the XX Valeria Victrix, one of the two legions stationed in Britain from the time of Claudius, for use closer to Rome.

In 407, Constantinius III became usurper-emperor of Britain and Gaul; when he went to the aid of Gaul he too removed substantial forces that were not replaced after his defeat.

A variety of historians date British independence from this episode. The Byzantine Procopius of Caesarea reports under the year 407:

64

And the island of Britain revolted from the Romans, and the soldiers there chose as their king Constantinus, a man of no mean station. And he straightway invaded both Spain and Gaul with great force, thinking to enslave these countries. . . . . And afterwards . . . . the army of the Visigoths under the leadership of Adaulphus proceeded into Gaul, and Constantinus, defeated in battle, died with his sons. However, the Romans never succeeded in recovering Britain, but it remained from that time on under tyrants.

In 409, Saxons appeared in formidable numbers. The historian Zosimus says the Britons raised fresh forces and repulsed this invasion themselves:

> The barbarians beyond the Rhine made such unbounded incursions over every province, as to reduce not only the Britons, but some of the Celtic nations also to the necessity of revolting from the empire, and living no longer under the Roman laws but as they themselves pleased. The Britons therefore took up arms, and incurred many daring enterprises for their own protection, until they had freed their cities from the barbarians who besieged them. In a similar manner, the whole of Armorica, with other provinces of Gaul, delivered themselves by the same means; expelling the Roman magistrates or officers, and erecting a government, such as they pleased, of their own.

Meanwhile, Alaric and his Goths were striding down the Italian peninsula to sack the city that if not eternal had for more than six hundred years been inviolate. Under the year 409, the *Anglo-Saxon Chronicle* says that Rome was "destroyed by the Goths 1110 years after it was built. Then after that the kings of the Romans no longer reigned in Britain. Altogether they had reigned there 470 years since Gaius Julius first came to the land."

It was in these circumstances, and against this background of preparation for authority, that the Romano-Britons took over. Yet in 410, they still felt themselves enough a part of the empire to send a fresh and urgent appeal for help to Honorius, Emperor of the West. He received it at Ravenna, huddled with his court out of the path of the invading Goths.

65

In replying, he had little choice. His message was succinct and final: "Let the communities look after themselves."

Romano-British leadership, military and civilian alike, was thus formally devolved on the shoulders of men who had previously been tribal administrators and ad hoc commanders. The Roman overlay was stripped off. Thereafter, the Britons' Atlantic island lay further and further beyond the horizon of imperial concern.

DARK AGE DUX BELLORUM

THE ROMAN WITHDRAWALS LEFT BRITAIN TRUNCATED OF HEAD and arm. Caradoc of Llancarvan, writing a history of these times in the mid-12th century, said:

> The reason that the British nation was at this time so weak and impotent, and so manifestly unable to withstand these barbarous enemies, who were far inferior as to the extent of the country, and probably in number of people, may in great measure be attributed to the ease and quietness the Britains enjoyed under the Roman government. For whilst the Roman legions continued in Britain, they ever undertook the security and preservation of it; so that the Britains . . . . quickly forgot that martial prowess, and military conduct which their ancestors so famously excelled in. For after their entire subjection to the Roman

empire they had little or no opportunity to experience their valour, excepting in some home-bred commotions, excited by the aspiring ambition of some male-contented gentlemen, which were quickly composed and reduced to nothing.

Even worse than this military weakness was the absence of a central government that could rally new strength. The group of leaders that must have combined to send the appeal to Honorius might have regarded themselves as legitimatized by his answer, but on the other hand, their failure to elicit help may have caused them to be quickly replaced.

A missive by a British Christian, *De Vita Christiana,* advising a young widow on her way of life, contains one of the political asides that occasionally give secular significance to tracts of the times. The author mentions with approval a recent revolution against the 'iudices', who may well have been the council that sent the appeal; it has brought to power an aristocratic government with officers dignified by time-honored Roman nomenclature.

Over the next years, unrest and social revolution were endemic in both Britain and Brittany. In Brittany, an egalitarian revolt set up a short-lived peasant republic. In Britain, similar anarchic upheavals seem to have brought the un-Romanized strata of society into conflict with the Romano-British at the same time that local scrambles for power were advancing tribal tyrants, subsequently legitimatized as kings and then ready to fight each other. Authority to undertake action beyond tribal boundaries, and especially to conduct military campaigns, had to be either negotiated multilaterally or grasped by force.

In the years between 417 and 425, the Roman military presence seems to have been temporarily restored in the southeast of the island: excavations at Rutupiae indicate early 5th century re-occupation. Under date of 418, the *Anglo-Saxon Chronicle* says: "In this year, the Romans collected all the treasures which were in Britain, and hid some in the ground, so that no one could find them afterwards, and took some with them into Gaul."

Even as late as 446, the Britons thought it worthwhile to appeal once again for Roman aid. An able Roman consul named Aetius had just achieved extensive military successes in the Breton peninsula, clearing it of invaders. The Britons urged him to cross the Channel and relieve their comparable misery. Several historians record the purport of a petition written in utter despair:

> Therefore again did the wretched remnants send a letter to Aetius, a powerful Roman. 'To Aetius, three times consul, the groans of the Britons: The barbarians drive us to the sea, and the sea drives us to the barbarians; between these two methods of death we are either massacred or drowned.'

But no help came. Thenceforth, the islanders were wholly on their own.

Meanwhile, invading Teutonic emigrants from the eastern shores of the North Sea effected new landings in various parts of the island. The Angles expanded the settlements that the Romans had permitted north and south of the Humber, and along with Frisians and Swabians occupied East Anglia. The Saxons swarmed into Kent and eventually into Essex, Sussex and Wessex. The Jutes appeared around the Isle of Wight.

The power that rode in the long-boats from the north can be judged from the funeral monument with its grave goods uncovered at Sutton Hoo near Woodbridge in Norfolk in 1939—a central chamber set amidships of an eighty-foot craft contained complete equipment for a warrior king. The king is thought to be Aethelhere of East Anglia: this is a pagan burial and he was one of the last of the Saxon pagans. The fact that he was killed or drowned at a battle in distant Yorkshire in 655 would account for the absence of a body: the grave goods were buried alone.

The equipment, now in the British Museum, includes a helmet, sword, and large round shield with a metal boss at its center; an iron standard topped by a bronze stag; a ceremonial whetstone carved at both ends in the shape of a man's head; two horns of the extinct

71

European aurochs fitted with metal bands as six-quart drinking vessels; a harp; enamelled gold brooches and buckles of exquisite handiwork; and a wealth of silver plate, among it a pair of spoons with 'Saulos' and 'Paulos' inscribed in Greek letters, and a twenty-seven inch Byzantine dish.

Since funeral rites follow immemorial tradition, those accorded Aethelhere can be taken as the same as those described in *Beowulf,* the Anglo-Saxon epic written in England less than fifty years later. From its accounts of two funerals, one a ship burial in which the body was sent out to sea, and one an interment in a funeral mound, the ceremony at Sutton Hoo can be reconstructed.

In the ship burial,

There stood at the haven   with rings on its prow
All sheeny and eager   the Atheling's bark.
Then they laid adown   the ruler beloved,
The giver of rings   in the lap of the ship,
The chief by the mast.   They brought there moreabove
Great store of things costly,   of treasure from far.
I never heard tell   of a keel fitted out
More fairly with weapons   and trappings of war,
With bills and with byrnies.   There lay on his breast
Of treasures a-many,   and these were to go
Far away, as a prize   for the ocean, with him.

And when Beowulf dies,

Then the people of the Wederas upheave
A barrow on the steep, which was high and broad,
Far to be sighted by men who pass the wave,
And had built in ten days that landmark for their lord:
Round what fire left they turned a sodded wall
As the wisest could plan it, most worthy of him and fair:
Into the mound they put ring, jewels,—all
That skilful work. . . .
They left it to earth to keep the precious lot
Gold under dust, where to this day it sits,
Not used by men. . . .
Then, out of them all, the princes rode their way
Round the barrow, valiant, twelve,
To speak their sorrow. . . .
. . . and say something of the man himself.

This was how Anglo-Saxons were honored in death. How they were housed in life has likewise been revealed, with the discovery of a royal palace of late pagan and early Christian times, occupied in the 6th and 7th centuries at Old Yeavering in northern Northumberland; it resembles the description in *Beowulf* of the Hall of Heorot. Against opponents of this level of culture the abandoned Romano-Britains now had to defend themselves.

Roman rule had, none the less, left a residue of resources and strategy. The effectiveness of a mobile army, striking now in one place, now in another, had been underscored by the successes of some of Rome's remedial reappearances in late years; it was facilitated by the network of Roman roads.

Furthermore, the history of the late empire recommended the use of cavalry. In 378, the army of Valens, Emperor of the East, suffered a military disaster at Adrianople in Thrace in which he himself was fatally wounded. His troops, arriving late, had been caught massed in the center of a plain, where mounted galloping tribesmen cut them down. In his *Decline and Fall of the Roman Empire,* Edward Gibbon grandiloquently affirms:

> The most skilful evolutions, the firmest courage, are scarcely sufficient to extricate a body of foot, encompassed, on an open plain, by a superior number of horse; but the troops of Valens, oppressed by the weight of the enemy and their own fears, were crowded into a narrow space, where it was impossible for them to extend their ranks, or even to use, with effect, their swords and javelins. . . . By the care of his attendants, Valens was removed from the field of battle to a neighbouring cottage, where they attemped to dress his wound and to provide for his future safety. But this humble retreat was instantly surrounded by the enemy; they tried to force the door . . . at length, impatient of delay, they set fire to a pile of dry faggots, and consumed the cottage with the Roman emperor and his train.

Thereafter, the eastern army developed a new form of cavalry, 75 mounted fighters with protective armor for both horse and rider, and the regular structure of the legion was modified to include more horsemen. Originally, only about 120 couriers and outriders had accompanied the 6600 foot soldiers of a full-strength legion, but the *Notitia Dignitatum,* an organization chart of the Roman military and civilian establishment privately compiled in the first quarter of the 5th century by a Roman civil servant who had squirreled away records of assorted dates, shows a ratio of 300 horse to 600 foot. The retinue attached to a British commander-in-chief, according to Welsh documents, usually comprised some 900 auxiliary horsemen in addition to the legion's complement. The Comes Britanniarum of late imperial times commanded six regiments of horse to three of foot.

Against Anglo-Saxon invaders, mounted men had an exceptional advantage, for this enemy possessed little armor and less cavalry. Procopius, whose military experience included campaigns in the West, derides their lack of horsemanship; writing in the first half of the sixth century, he says:

> . . . they enter battle on foot. And this is not merely because they are unpractised in horsemanship, but the fact is that they do not even know what a horse is, since they never see even so much as a picture of a horse. . . . And whenever it happens that some of them on an embassy or some other mission make a visit among the Romans or the Franks or any other nation which has horses, and they are constrained to ride on horseback, they are altogether unable to leap upon their backs, but other men lift them in the air and thus mount them on the horses, and when they wish to get off, they are again lifted and placed on the ground.

The post-Roman defenders of Britain therefore had special incentive to develop a mobile mounted force.

Excavations at the fort of Trimontium (Newstead) have indicated that they not only did so but bred a strain of heavy horses to add power to their charge. Finds at this site, most of them now in the Archaeological Museum in Edinburgh, included two distinct types and sizes of horse skeletons. One resembled the coarse-limbed little native moor ponies. The other, much larger, stood some 12.2 hands high; its slender legs were like those of horses of Arab ancestry.

Early 5th century British history likewise instanced at least one assumption of command by a free-lance leader that brought results comparable to those of the Roman special missions of late years.

In 429, St. Germanus (the St. Harmon of Wales, the St. Germain of his bishopric at Auxerre) came to Britain to help refute the Pelagian heresy. Pelagius was a Celtic Christian living in Rome who believed that good can be attained through the exercise of human will independent of divine grace. This view, which clashed with the teaching of St. Augustine, caused him and an Irish companion Coelestius to be banished from Rome in 418; it was again condemned by the Council of Ephesus in 431.

Since Pelagius' doctrine had attracted a considerable following in Gaul and Italy, and an even larger one in Britain, Germanus was sent to scotch the heresy at its source. While he was in Wales, a combined force of Saxons and Picts intruded. Earlier in life, the saint had been Governor of Brittany and military commander on the Gallic Channel coast. He now took charge of the available forces at a battle near Mold in Flintshire. He terrified the astonished enemy by ordering a rolling cry of 'Alleluia!' as his men charged, and administered a resounding defeat.

Germanus apparently found that Pelagianism had powerful support in the person of a recently emerged paramount king. At the end of the first quarter of the 5th century, Vortigern (the name means overlord) came to power in Wales, and by 425 had accumulated control over much of the island. He is said to have been the son-in-law of the usurper-emperor Maximus; his ancestry included Roman names. Yet whether he ruled as heir to the Roman departure, or as leader of tribal revolt was its final cause is uncertain.

Shortly, he is found searching for allies against the Picts, and inviting in the Saxons, awarding them lands in Kent at a safe distance from his center of power. While Roman history provided parallels on the northeast coast around the Humber, this particular

77

arrangement gave a foothold to powerful contingents that soon fell out with their sponsor.

The Anglo-Saxon Chronicle reports this Saxon arrival under the year 449, but it may have occurred as much as two decades earlier, since Vortigern is thought to have begun his reign around 425. The entry reads:

> In this year Mauritius and Valentinus* succeeded to the throne and ruled for seven years. And in their days Vortigern invited the English hither, and they then came in three ships to Britain at the place Ebbsfleet. King Vortigern gave them land in the south-east of this island on condition that they should fight against the Picts. They then fought against the Picts and had the victory wherever they came. They then sent to Angeln, bidding them send more help, and had them informed of the cowardice of the Britons and the excellence of the land. . . . . Their leaders were two brothers, Hengist and Horsa, who were the sons of Wihtgils.

* Actually, Valentinus III became Emperor of the West in 425; Marcianus became Emperor of the East in 450.

Within six years, Hengist and Horsa are reported in revolt against the British; the *Chronicle* declares that though Horsa was killed, Hengist and his line continued from strength to strength: in 456, "the Britons then deserted Kent and fled with great fear to London"; in 473, the Anglo-Saxons "captured countless spoils and the Britons fled from the English as from fire." Once the fertile southeast corner of the island was permanently secured, its new occupants pressed westward.

Evidence on the geography of the British resistance during the second half of the 5th and the early years of the 6th century, with possible sites of some of the battles that culminated in a reversal of the Anglo-Saxon inflow, is shown by the map on page 69. The pages that follow present currently available data on the historic Arthur, on the engagements that he captained and the British leaders of his time, political and military.

Two types of factual source are at hand: writings on various subjects by his contemporaries and near-contemporaries, and the intensive research of the present period. From the ancient documents, often discursive and imprecise, scraps of relevant information can be gleaned here and there, sometimes in unlikely places. In occasional manuscripts, cramped columns display a more connected chronicle. Modern findings, some turned up by the spade, some dated by radioisotopes, some observed by scrutiny of ancient and newly identified manuscript sources, sometimes contradict ancient affirmations, and at other times sustain and expand them. Even amidst increasing sureties, for every announced date and place there is apt to be a more or less persuasive variant, for every conjecture a counter-conjecture. The current state of the archaeological-historical art can be seen in the following summaries.

THE ANCIENT SOURCES

bout 540, the Celtic monk, Gildas, though writing primarily to castigate the wickedness of five contemporary Welsh and West Country kings, includes the earliest known account of events of the preceding century. He called his book *The Loss and Conquest of Britain*. Not very much is known of Gildas' life, but a 12th century biographer says that he was born in Scotland, lived in Wales, evangelized in Brittany, and died there. His history begins with a description of Britain:

This island, stiff-necked and stubborn-minded, from the time of its being first inhabited, ungratefully rebels, sometimes against God, sometimes against her own citizens, and frequently, also, against foreign kings and their subjects.

After detailing the occupation by which the Romans "imposed

79

submission on our island," and left taskmasters under whom all money, "whether bronze or copper, gold or silver, was stamped with Caesar's image," he enumerates early incursions of Scots and Picts, and the appeals made by British envoys "like timorous chickens, crowding under the protecting wings of their parents" until the Romans "left the country, giving notice that they could no longer be harassed by such laborious expeditions."

Thereafter, the Saxons were called in by a leader whom Gildas identifies only as a "proud tyrant" but who is certainly Vortigern. Some years later, the Romano-Britons mounted a new effort at self-defense:

> the poor remnants of our nation . . . . that they might not be brought to utter destruction, took arms under the conduct of Ambrosius Aurelianus, a modest man, who of all the Roman nation was then alone in the confusion of this troubled period by chance left alive. His parents, who for their merit were adorned with the purple, had been slain in these same broils, and now his progeny, in these our days, although shamefully degenerated from the worthiness of their ancestors, provoke to battle their cruel conquerors, and by the goodness of our Lord obtain the victory.
>
> After this, sometimes our countrymen, sometimes the enemy, won the field, to the end that our Lord might in this land try after his accustomed manner these his Israelites, whether they loved him or not, until the year of the siege of Bath-Hill (Mons Badonicus) when took place also the last almost, though not the least slaughter of our cruel foes, which was (as I am sure) forty-four years and one month after the landing of the Saxons, and also the time of my own nativity.

The passage gives a name, Ambrosius Aurelianus, to the organizer of Romano-British resistance. It also enables computation of a date for the battle of Badon. Since Gildas is thought to have written about 540, both his probable birth date and the date given for the Saxon arrival in their *Chronicle* would put the battle a little before 500. Gildas does not name the leader of the British forces at Badon.

hronicles that do name him began to be compiled somewhat later; about 830, the Welsh monk Nennius prepared a new edition of an existing *History of the Britons,* "compiled in the 858th year of our Lord's incarnation and the 24th of Mervin King of Britain." The year-by-year chronology, *The Annals of the Britons,* was attached to this manuscript about a hundred years later.

After reviewing the Roman occupation, Nennius treats the unsettled period from which Vortigern emerged with his invitation to the Saxons; he says that Vortigern's son Vortimer died while trying to dislodge the newcomers from Kent. In the period when the tribes were fighting among themselves, his chronology mentions an Ambrosius (perhaps the father "adorned with the purple" of Aurelianus): "there are twelve years from the reign of Vortigern to the quarrel of Guitolin and Ambrosius, that is Guoloppum, the battle of Guoloph." Guoloph is thought to be the present Wallop in Hampshire; only a few miles northwest is the town of Amesbury, sometimes spelled Ambresbury, in Wiltshire, that was probably named for Ambrosius.

The passage in which Nennius recounts the turning of the Saxon tide introduces Arthur and names his victories:

At that time, the Saxons were waxing strong in number and were increasing in Britain.

When Hengist was dead, Octha, his son, passed over from the north part of Britain to the kingdom of the Kentishmen and from him are sprung the kings of the Kentishmen.

Then it was that Arthur was wont to fight against them in those days along with the kings of the Britons, but he himself was dux bellorum, leader of battles. The first battle was at the mouth of the river which is called Gleni. The second, third, fourth and fifth, on another river, which is called Dubglas, and is in the region of Linnuis. The sixth battle was on the river which is called Bassas. The seventh was a battle in the wood of Celidon, that is Cat Coit Celidon. The eighth was the battle at Castellum Guinnion, in which Arthur carried the image of Saint Mary, ever Virgin, on his shoulders, and the pagans were put to flight on that day and there was a great slaughter of them through the power of our Lord Jesus Christ and through the power of saint Mary the Virgin, his mother. The ninth battle was fought at the City of the Legion. The tenth battle he fought on the river, which is called Trebuit. The eleventh occurred on the mountain, which is called Agned. The twelfth was the battle on Mount Badon, in which there fell together in one day 960 men in one onset of Arthur, and no one laid them low save himself alone. And in all the battles he remained victor.

The name Arthur was unusual at the time. If its derivation was Latin, there had been a 2nd century Roman commander of the VI Victrix, Lucius Artorius Castus. If its derivation was Celtic, it might have come from the word 'arth' — bear; Gildas, when specifying the evil ways of his five kings, mentions that one of them had been "charioteer to the Bear."

Not enough is known to say whether Arthur, like Ambrosius Aurelianus, came from the Roman or Romanized families remaining on the island, or whether he represented the un-Romanized tribal talent that these years brought to the top. Considerable regrouping undoubtedly took place as the Anglo-Saxon advance penetrated inland from the island's southern and eastern shores. Tribes on the periphery of the former Roman province, that previously had fought the Romans, now had incentive to make common cause with Romano-Britons who while defending the old way of life were repelling this new invasion. They certainly supplied military manpower and at least some of the military leadership that went with it.

ther authors repeat Gildas and Nennius, with additions. An 8th century English version of these events, the Venerable Bede's *Ecclesiastical History of the English Nation,* largely copies Gildas while inserting a few dates. Under 447, he notes that "the Britons, being for a time delivered from foreign wars, wasted themselves by civil wars, and then gave themselves up to more heinous crimes." He dates Ambrosius Aurelianus' leadership at 466, and Badon at about 493.

A final reference in the 10th century chronology appended to Nennius closes the Dark Age account. After giving the date of Badon as 516, a laconic notation sets 537 as the year of the internecine engagement that closed Arthur's career: "The action of Camlann, in which Arthur and Medrault fell. And there was a pestilence in Britain and Ireland."

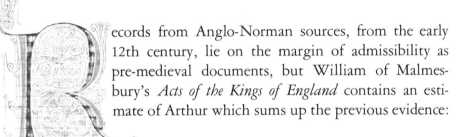

Records from Anglo-Norman sources, from the early 12th century, lie on the margin of admissibility as pre-medieval documents, but William of Malmesbury's *Acts of the Kings of England* contains an estimate of Arthur which sums up the previous evidence:

When Vortimer was dead, the strength of the Britons became exhausted and their hopes dwindled and faded away. Indeed, they would have come to an end then and there had not Ambrosius the last of the Romans, who was king after Vortigern, harried the hordes of the barbarians through the glorious work of the warrior Arthur.

This is that Arthur about whom we hear so much nonsense from British sources nowadays. And yet he deserves the fame which only true history can bestow, instead of the dreams of unreliable legends; for he saved his countrymen from collapse for many years, and roused their courage to endurance and to war.

RECENT FINDINGS

The compilers of the early chronicles faced a formidable task. They were men who had to try to make a sensible sequence out of

83

what they heard tell; to sort an accumulated pile of memories of a troubled century and order its episodes into a chain of events. Since their time, generations of antiquarians and scholars, and more recently archaeologists, have also worried these scanty bones.

Winston Churchill, in his *Birth of Britain,* dismisses the tentativeness of some of the more modern scholarship with a characteristic snort. After an exemplary quote from an historian who will go no further on the historicity of Arthur than to venture the opinion that "it is reasonably certain that a petty chieftain named Arthur did exist, probably in South Wales . . . . ." Churchill growls: "This is not much to show after so much toil and learning."

More toil and learning, out-of-doors as well as in studies, is currently being applied to places where Arthur is said to have lived, to have died, to have battled.

South Cadbury, the Iron Age hill fort at Sparkford near Queen Camel in Somerset, has been traditionally known as Camelot. A thorough archaeological investigation is now in progress and has uncovered Dark Age artifacts impressive enough to establish use by a ranking personage of that period.

Human occupancy here has a long record. Located on the site of a Neolithic causewayed enclosure, South Cadbury is one of the few hill forts in all Britain to have four rings of rampart and ditch. Entrances give access from east, west and south.

Saxon occupancy after the Dark Age is evidenced by fortification walls and buildings. Nearby Somerton was the residence of the West Saxon kings, and one of their numerous mints in Somerset issued coins marked Cadanbyrig under Aethelred II and Canute, c. 1010–20.

Beginning in Henry VIII's time, records of visits by antiquarians are almost continuous. On official assignment from the king, John Leland prepared the *Itinerary* of painstaking travel during 1543–46 that makes him the Pausanias of the Tudor world. In 1544 he wrote 84 a treatise, *Assertio inclytissimi Arturij Regis Britanniae,* with lists of foreign and domestic authors who mention Arthur, in which he extols

this site as "Camaletum castrum olim magnificentissimum" and reports the finding of "much gold, sylver and coper of the Romayne coynes and many antique thinges" within its precincts. A quarter of a century later, William Camden likewise identified the hill as Camelot.

Elizabethan maps show the place-name Camelleck; Drayton, Stow, and Speed in the 16th–17th century, and Musgrave and Stukeley in the early 18th, all visited it. In Stukeley's *Itinerarium Curiosum* of 1724 there is mention of pavements and arches; and "in this camp they find many pebble stones exactly round, half a peck at a time; whereas there are none such in the country: they suppose them stones to sling withal, fetched from the sea." A cemetery by the west gate, containing skeletons of men and boys, shows that some died slinging.

Nineteenth century antiquaries dug and found a deep shaft containing many bronze bracelets, rings and beads similar to those offered as votives at Romano-British temples. Further probes were made in

ASSERTIO

imperij dignitate filio notho, quod legitimũ non ha-
beret.

Corona Arturij.

Ritannica adfirmat historia Ar-
turium insulis regni decimo quin
to ætatis suæ anno initiatũ fuisse à
Dubritio vrbis Legionum epis-
copo. Ioannes Aureæ scriptor
historiæ videtur octodecim ad-
numerare annos Arturio regiam
sedem conscendenti. Scalæchronica, cuius libri, vt cõ
iectura ducor, quidam Graius autor fuit, aiunt Artu-
rium coronæ insignia Ventæ accepisse. Pictorum &
Scottorum duo reguli Lotho, cui Anna soror Aurē-
lij Ambrosij regis Britannorum nupserat, & Conra-
nus cui Ada soror Annæ coniunx data fuerat, cœpe-
runt tàm lætis Arturij successibus inuidere: nam v-
terque, sed præcipuè Lotho, ad Britanniæ imperium
aspirabat. Hinc factum postea vt ille, adiuncto sibi
Osca, alias Occa homine impurissimo, bellũ Arturio intulerit. Tandem ad manus peruentũ est, victusꝗ
Pictus peioreis partes tulit, partim Hoeli inuictissimi
præsidio, qui tunc ducem ibi agebat. Libellus de impe-
rio Britannorum, & Anglorum in Scottos beneficia-
rios adfirmat hanc victoriam Eboraci ab Hoelo par-
tam: vtꝗ deuictis Scottis antiquas sedes precibus mo
tus Arturius reliquerit sub Augusello suo, quèm eis
regulum præfecit. Nꝗc sors melior Saxones excepit,
interfecto Colgrino duce, Baldrico autem, & Chel-
drico fugientibus. Victoriam secuta est concordia.
Lotho se Britanno dedidit. Mordredus, & Gallo-
ambie

the first decades of this century. At the same time, much folklore was collected in the surrounding villages, where elders affirmed that Arthur often visited the area. The Neolithic causeway running northwest towards Glastonbury—on a clear evening, Glastonbury Tor is visible from the hill ramparts—was known as King Arthur's Lane and existed as a bridle path until the 1890's. Villagers claimed that Arthur and his ghostly riders water their horses on Christmas Eve at a spring near Sutton Montis southwest of the hill, where a silver horseshoe was found. The hill was believed to be hollow: one old countryman expressed the wish that one of the new railroads would come this way and run a tunnel into it; another, who held Arthur to be buried there, greeted the leader of a group of investigators with the anxious query: "Oh, sir, have you come to take him away?"

Then in 1966, scientific examination of the area began. Geophysical soundings, corroborated by aerial photography, determined initial choice of areas: the first three campaigns identified occupation in the early Neolithic, late Bronze and pre-Roman Iron Age, and by Britons and Saxons in the post-Roman period.

Among buildings so far explored, a cruciform structure, interpreted as a church, dates possibly from the 5th–6th century, but probably from the Late Saxon town. In 1968, firm evidence of a 6th century hall appeared: the foundation, cut into solid rock, with slots for upright timbers of a thirty-five foot wall. In the soil tamped round the posts a 6th-century amphora fragment showed that persons living here imported Mediterranean wine.

But most telling is the new fortification, by post-Roman builders using pre-Roman technique, above ramparts grass-grown since the Roman conquest. In some places four courses high, it is slotted for breastwork timbers. Dig director Leslie Alcock of the University of Wales, comparing other late 5th century forts, says: "Cadbury by contrast is a strong pre-Roman fort, formidable even in decay but none the less forcefully refortified. It is very tempting to think that it must have played a special role in the military affairs of southern England in the generations around A.D. 500."

87

Evidence will thus shortly be at hand regarding a place where

Arthur is supposed to have lived. Widely separated localities compete, without substantiation, as scenes of his death.

The Glastonbury legends will be considered later. A Cornish tradition locates Camlann at Slaughter Bridge on the Camel River near Camelford, relying on Leland's statement that "pieces of armour, rings, and brass furniture for horses are sometimes digged up here by countrymen," and that "Arthur, the British Hector," killed Modred on the bridge, Modred having first wounded him with a poisoned sword; Arthur then withdrew upstream to die at the edge of the water where an incised stone marks the spot.

Richard Carew reports the stone again in 1602 in his *Survey of Cornwall,* and it is still beside the stream. A path through a pasture leads to a steep bank where a fallen plane tree bridges the water with slippery footing; the stone lies below. But the inscription on it does not concern Arthur: it has been deciphered as "Latini ic jacit filius Mogari."

The attribution of this site confuses Camlann with the defeat inflicted on the Britons at Slaughter Bridge in 823, at the end of the Saxon conquest of Cornwall.

Other sources envisage the engagement of Modred and Arthur in the north. In Scotland, the Roman town of Camelon on the Antonine Wall west of Falkirk is one proposed site because a monument on the opposite bank of the Carron River was known as Furness Arthur in 1293 and the place has since been called Arthur's Oven.

More serious consideration is given to the likelihood that Camlann—the name means 'crooked enclosure'—may have been an elision of Camboglanna, the fort on Hadrian's Wall at Birdoswald.

But more important to history, if not to romance, than the places where Arthur lost are the places where he won, especially Badon.

Ancient writers placed the siege at Bath, and while the site seems far west, Solsbury Hill, just northeast of the city, is a hill fort with slopes and ramparts suitable for cavalry.

Modern scholars constantly re-fight the battle of the battles, but only a few of the names on Nennius' list can be identified with assurance. It is, however, worth noting that many of them took place on the banks of rivers: the odds would favor a cavalry attack at a ford on floundering foot-soldiers splashing through a stream.

In his *Britannia,* in the Harvard *History of the Provinces of the Roman Empire,* Sheppard Frere says,

Down, then, to 442 Vortigern successfully maintained the independence of Britain. But the rebellion of his Germanic federates introduced a period of chaos fatal to the villa system and destructive to Vortigern's own supremacy. In the latter 5th century the leadership passed to Ambrosius Aurelianus and after him to Arthur. Little is known of either. Ambrosius appears in the pages of Gildas, but Arthur does not, and his actions and personality are almost impenetrably overlaid by medieval romance. The evidence is sufficient to allow belief that he had a real existence and that he was probably the victor of Mount Badon. It is likely that he succeeded Ambrosius in the leadership; indeed, he is called dux bellorum in the Historia Brittonum, which suggests a memory of late Roman military titles, and may indicate some sort of unified command arranged between several petty kingdoms. Using mounted forces, these leaders were able to strike back at the Saxons, who had little body armour and inferior weapons. The use of cavalry enabled unexpected blows to be struck from distant bases, and it was a form of warfare in which small numbers of horsemen could rout many times their number of ill-armed barbarian foot-soldiers. It is perhaps no coincidence that eight out of the twelve battles traditionally associated with Arthur were fought at fords, and so were other 5th century battles; a well-planned charge by even a few horsemen on a force of foot soldiers crossing a stream could be expected to produce maximum confusion.

The 'City of the Legion' is surely either Chester or Caerleon. The forest of Celidon still exists in Scotland. Linnuis may have been Lincoln. But after these have been checked off, doubt sets in. In the surer days of the 19th century, some scholars insisted that Nennius puts all the battles above the Wall—"regiones que sunt in aquilone juxta murum qui vocatur Gual"—and one of them identified the lot in a consecutive strategy. But 20th century authorities are tentative.

That some of the battles should be in the upper parts of the highland zone seems self-evident, even if the forest of Celidon were less identifiable today. But while in Roman times most of the troubles in that perennially troubled area were due to downward thrusts from the north, in the Dark Age some of them were due to upward thrusts from the Anglo-Saxon kingdoms around the Humber, expanding their holdings as new immigrants arrived.

A series of earthworks built in Yorkshire at this time shows the expectation of such attacks: the Becca Banks face south, keeping watch on movement up the Great North Road; Scots Dyke faces east on the left-hand fork of that road above Scots Corner.

Welsh literature corroborates the need for such defense. Just below Scots Dyke is Catraeth (Catterick), where the Angles administered a punishing blow around 590. A major coalition of British chiefs and their forces went out to resist them there, including the Goddodin, the tribe who held the east coast from Hadrian's Wall to Edinburgh.

The engagement was a disaster, lamented in the epic, *Goddodin,* which names, one by one, the 6th century heroes who fell there. One line offers a poignant memorial to Arthur; it praises the prowess of a warrior who "glutted the black ravens on the wall of the city, even though he was no Arthur."

Catraeth ended combined British resistance in the north. The battle was as definitive for this region as the prior engagement when the Anglo-Saxons drove a wedge between South Wales and Cornwall at Dyrham in 577, and their victory that cut Strathclyde off from North Wales at Chester in 616.

But in the latter 5th century, the British had not been driven nearly that far back, and the northern frontier probably appeared a secondary consideration: more pressing was the defense of the fertile stretches of Wiltshire and Somerset toward which the Saxons from Kent and Wessex had begun to push. Accordingly, many modern historians have put the site of Badon in one or the other of two positions in south central Britain, Badbury Rings near Wimborne in Dorset or the area near the Swindon Gap in Berkshire and Wiltshire.

In both areas, Iron Age hill forts contain evidence of re-occupation in the 5th to 6th century. Badbury Rings is impressive with its three concentric circles of rampart and ditch. It is not far from Charford, mentioned as a battle site in the *Anglo-Saxon Chronicle*. A still clearly-defined Roman road connects it with the fort of Old Sarum above Salisbury, where the Britons were defeated in 552. If the Saxons attempted to move straight west from Kent, Badbury Rings would have been a probable objective, a formidable obstacle that could be turned into a highly advantageous possession.

But the Saxons are known to have begun colonization of the Upper Thames by the close of the 5th century; it is also possible that they might have undertaken an enveloping movement to descend on the Britons through the Swindon Gap in the Chiltern Hills. The

Wansdyke, the great north-facing ditched fortification, complete by the end of the 5th century, that runs in an east-west line from Savernake Forest southeast of Marlborough to the south bank of the Avon west of Bath, was clearly built with protection against an enemy coming from the north in mind.

The Iron Age fort called Badbury between Highworth and Faringdon in Berkshire would have permitted defenders a sweeping surveillance of the Thames Valley. A few miles south, above Badbury village and north of the Wansdyke, Liddington fort rises 911 feet above sea level. It monitors the Icknield Way as it arrives from the east on the crest of high ground, and commands the Roman road coming south through the Swindon Gap. For surprise deployment of cavalry, the slopes surrounding it are very suitable.

The Swindon Gap defenses are not in themselves as formidable as Badbury Rings, but they are exceptionally well located: from Liddington, a system of smoke signals by day and fire by night could have alerted Uffington in the Valley of the White Horse, Ranbury in

94

Gloucestershire, and a sequence of forts in Wiltshire. It is also worth noting that rather more than a half-century later, the Saxons are known to have attacked in this area. In 556, at the hill fort of Barbury only slightly further west, they administered a punishing defeat, one

95

of a series culminating in the battle of Dyrham, when they gained control of Gloucester, Cirencester and Bath.

Wherever Badon was fought, the salient fact about it is that British tribal kings, defending the residue of Roman Britain under the leadership of a dux bellorum named Arthur, inflicted at that battle a startling repulse of the Saxon invasion.

Even the *Anglo-Saxon Chronicle* ceases for a time its claims of victories, filling the empty years with occasional notations of eclipses of the sun.

Forty-four years after Badon, the ensuing peace still held: Gildas was ascribing the degeneration of his fellow-countrymen to the fact that they "had never experienced the troubles, and knew only our present security . . . . now that our foreign wars are over."

Contemporary scholarship has reached the view that at Badon, for the first and only time in the Britons' rear-guard fight, the Saxon invaders were not only checked but thrown back so vigorously that considerable numbers of them left the island. C. E. Stevens of Magdalen College, Oxford, points out that this reverse migration is unique in the long history of barbarian incursions into the provinces of Rome.

The resulting deflection of the Saxon thrust to Belgium and France is attested by both documentary and archaeological evidence. Procopius notes just as Gildas did the durability of the recent peace; accretions of Saxon population and place names occur in Belgium and France just when numbers are dwindling in Britain.

Contraction of the Saxon communities in both Norfolk and Kent is archaeologically demonstrable; the few settlers who continued in Britain when their fellows returned to the Continent lived in fear.

It was the turn of the Saxons to build defensive dykes. Peter Hunter Blair, of Emmanuel College, Cambridge, in his *Roman Britain and Early England* says:

96

There was a time when men living in East Anglia sought to bar free passage along the Icknield Way by the construction of a series of de-

fensive dykes which cut transversely across it, dykes which were designed to give protection against an enemy approaching from the south-west. These barriers, of which the Devil's Dyke on Newmarket Heath remains the most impressive, though in their day Fleam Dyke and Heydon Dyke were not less so, still present us with a puzzle. Yet they may seem to some to be appropriate to an age in which a prolonged period of warfare between the native British defenders and the invading Anglo-Saxons, culminating in a great British victory, had brought the progress of the invasions to a temporary halt and thrown some of the invaders back upon the eastern parts of the country, where they might have greater security before moving over to attack once again. Such an age occurred after the British victory at Mons Badonicus.

THE REALMS OF ARTHUR

John R. Morris, of the University of London, who has specialized in Dark Age dating, both as evidenced in historical records and as revealed by excavations, and whose forthcoming major work is titled *The Age of Arthur,* has examined the grave goods in Anglo-Saxon cemeteries in England and on the Continent. He says:

> There is clear evidence, documentary and archaeological, of a reverse migration of Anglo-Saxons to Europe. English Saxons were held in the 9th century to have played a considerable part in the growth of modern, inland, Saxony; they received land in modern Belgium as mercenary allies of the Frankish kings, and they fought wars upon the Rhine. There is plenty of Saxon pottery in a great Frankish cemetery at Anderlecht (Brussels) and plenty of Kentish jewellery at Herpes in southwestern France; in northeastern France, there is a scatter of purely Saxon place-names, with a number of cruciform brooches of the first half of the sixth century (Aberg's groups III and IV) to accompany them, but none earlier or later. It would appear that the effect of the British victory was to contain the Anglo-Saxon settlers within their previous limits, if not to reduce those limits, and to coerce their increasing population either to emigrate overseas or to expand within existing territories.

Here, it is submitted, is the origin and source of the Arthurian charisma. Arthur was the one military leader of his time who was able to send the invaders back across the sea. In an era when the Roman empire was everywhere crumbling, he summoned the strength necessary to give one of its provinces a final autumn interval. It was borrowed time, but it lasted twice as long as that between the early 20th century's two world wars.

Such a victory is the stuff of which myths are made, songs memorized. The remaining chapters of this book explore the rise of the epic through which Arthur the man became Arthur the hero, and the imaginary realms with which he was endowed from place to place and from period to period.

IV

CELTIC
ORIGINS

HUMAN POWERS AND MAGIC ATTRIBUTES BLEND IN THE MEMORIES and fantasies attached to the chief Arthurian characters in the Celtic West. In this, Arthur's earliest realm, historic leaders become one with folk heroes and gods of ancient mythology. Many of the places associated with their names in Wales, Devon and Cornwall belong at one and the same time to the history of the Dark Age and to its imagination.

For centuries, the Celts of highland Britain had no written language. Their bards were their collective memory. These were no less learned men because their learning was oral. Admission into their fraternity was measured both by linguistic skill and by prodigious feats of recitation. Their monopoly as custodians of their people's tradition, though diminished when manuscript versions of their uttered literature began to be inscribed during the 9th to 11th centuries, was not destroyed until the coming of printed books.

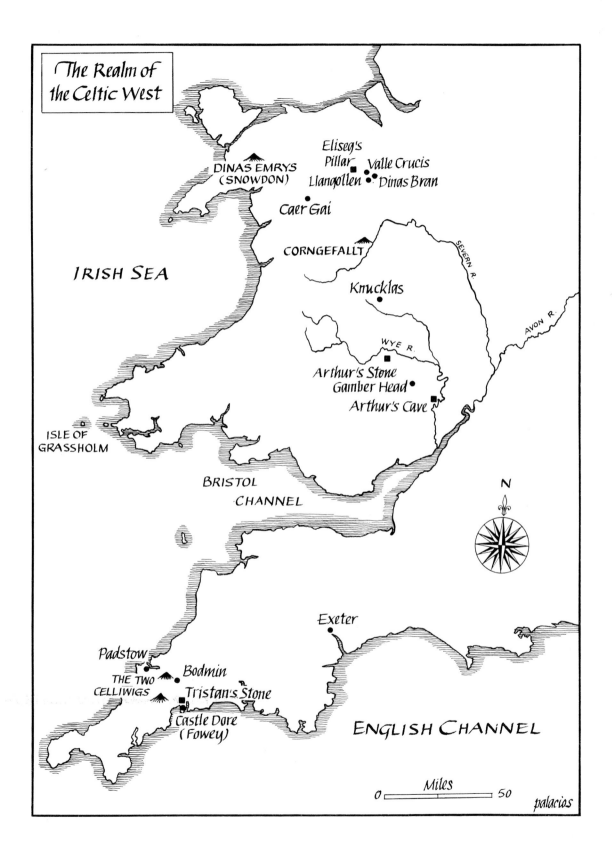

The Realm of the Celtic West

DINAS EMRYS (SNOWDON)

Eliseg's Pillar
Valle Crucis
Llangollen
Dinas Bran

Caer Gai

CORNGEFALLT

IRISH SEA

Knucklas

SEVERN R.

AVON R.

WYE R.

Arthur's Stone
Gamber Head
Arthur's Cave

ISLE OF GRASSHOLM

BRISTOL CHANNEL

N

Exeter

Padstow
Bodmin
THE TWO CELLIWIGS
Tristan's Stone
Castle Dore (Fowey)

ENGLISH CHANNEL

Miles
0   50

palacios

In the outpourings of an art that passed from voice to voice for more than a half-millennium it is hard to tell what is early and what is late. The transmitted mythology, stories and history must have changed with the years, but when and how? Then too, in an orally transmitted literature, the losses are incalculable: what is not repeated, disappears.

Yet fragmentary though they are, the Celtic writings available today pass on a delightful collection of early records, beliefs and fantasies expressed by contemporaries or near-contemporaries of Arthur's time. Two of the four early poets whose names are known, Aneurin and Taliesin, are thought to have lived in the 6th century.

Within the Welsh literary profession, distinctions existed between the bards, who were dignified repositories of the people's immemorial record, and the storytellers, whose relation to the bards was that of popularizer to scholar; since the latter recited for entertainment, their offerings moved easily from history to marvel to romance. The duty of the bard was to remind his hearers of what had happened. The pleasure of the storyteller was to astonish them with a tall tale.

The distinctive bardic medium for recalling facts was the three-line triad—a definitive collection of the *Trioedd Ynys Prydein—Triads of the Island of Britain* has recently been issued by the University of Wales. But the bards also wrote poems, exalting living heroes and lamenting those who fell.

The tales of the storytellers were in prose; they began to be written down by the 12th century and translations into English have become increasingly available since Lady Charlotte Guest undertook her *Mabinogion* in the 1840's.

By good fortune, both the sketchy accuracy of the triad and the colorful fecklessness of the tale are at hand with respect to an incident that was a prologue to events of Arthur's day, and in addition, there is testimony about it in Roman records and on an ancient Welsh monument.

The incident concerned the weakening of Britain in late Roman times by an imperial rival who took troops across the Channel and lost them in defeat.

The triad recalls three British armies that found a point of no return in Gaul; as leader of the second force it lists Maxen Wledig, "and they never returned to this Island." 'Wledig' means head of state; this Maxen is the Magnus Clemens Maximus whom British legions proclaimed emperor in 383.

Roman records show that he stripped the Wall of troops and went to France. There, he defeated and killed his rival emperor, Gratian. But five years later, fighting near the head of the Adriatic, he in turn was defeated and killed by the Emperor Theodosius I. The survivors of his forsaken army are thought to have begun the British colonization of Brittany.

Political and military affairs did not trouble the storytellers: in a highly favorable literary glimpse, *The Dream of Macsen Wledig* announces him as "Emperor of Rome, and he was the handsomest and wisest of men, and the best fitted to be emperor."

The glamor of the storyteller and the facts of history are combined in the inscription on one of the most venerable of Welsh stones, dating from the mid-9th century, the Pillar of Eliseg near Llangollen. This patriotic monument, formerly topped by the cross from which Valle Crucis and its Abbey took their name, was re-erected in 1779. Carved on it is a genealogy of the old royal line of the Welsh kingdom of Powys; in 1696, while it was still lying prone after desecration, its lettering was deciphered and parts can be dimly made out still. It attests that Maxen was Vortigern's father-in-law.

Like all patriotic monuments, this one avoids unpleasant references: it extols "Britu, son of Vortigern, whom Germanus blessed, and who was born of Seuira, daughter of Maximus, the king who killed the king of the Romans."

These glimpses of an historic incident vouchsafed by text and artifact illustrate the disjointedness of transmission through Celtic sources. Like a Welsh landscape on a windy day of alternate mist and sun, persons and events appear and disappear. It is the same with the chief characters of the Arthurian legend: one by one, for a moment, they stand revealed in the clarity of intense observation; the next moment, they are shrouded in obscurity.

103

Though the Celtic realm of Arthur is a realm of lights and shadows, all of his early companions are displayed, in brief flashes, in its literature. Their settings are the homely surroundings of an agricultural people. Arthur himself is a rough and ready chieftain who wrests his bride from a giant and gathers round him fighters who are fit—and ripe—for a harrying.

His foremost warrior is his nephew Gawain (Gwalchmei) whom triads praise among the Three Fearless Men, the Three Well-Endowed Men, the Three Men of the Island of Britain who were most courteous to Guests and Strangers. Early in the 12th century, William of Malmesbury, announcing that his grave had just been found at Ross in Pembrokeshire, called him

> A warrior most renowned for his valour, he was expelled from his kingdom by the brother and nephew of Hengist . . . . . but not until he had compensated for his exile by much damage wrought upon them, worthily sharing in the praise of his uncle, in that they deferred for many years the ruin of their falling country.

As late as the second half of the 14th century, a midland author made him the hero of *Sir Gawain and the Green Knight.*

All versions of the Arthurian cycle name two constant companions of Arthur's household: his seneschal, spelled Kay in later accounts and Kei or Cei by Welsh writers, and his butler, Bedivere— Bedwyr to the bards.

It was to Kay's father that King Uther Pendragon confided the new-born Arthur to be raised as his own son. (Displaced at his mother's breast, Kay always stammered.) As the scene of Arthur's childhood, therefore, Welshmen point to the hill fort known as Caer Gai above the River Dee west of Bala in Merionethshire.

From this height, only twenty-five miles from the Irish Sea, majestic views sweep down over Lake Bala and across to the twin peaks of Aran Benllyn. Inscriptions in the Cardiff museum show that two cohorts of the XX Valeria Victrix were based here in Roman days; for the past four hundred years, an Elizabethan house, the center of a farmstead, has stood within the walls of their fortlet on the hill.

In one of the longer Celtic poems, Arthur expands on the exploits of Bedwyr and Kay when challenged by a forbidding porter at the gate of a castle:

> *On Eidyn's mountain*
> *He combated with champions,*
> *By the hundred they fell—*
> *They fell a hundred at a time*

105

Before Bedwyr . . . .
On the shores of Tryvrwd;
Combating with Garwlwyd,
Victorious was his wrath
Both with sword and shield.
It were vain to boast
Against Kei in battle.
His sword in battle was
Not to be pledged from his hand . . . . .
Before the kings of Emrys
I have seen Kei in haste.
Leader of the harryings,
Long would he be in his wrath;
Heavy was he in his vengeance;
Terrible in his fighting.
When from a horn he drank
He drank as much as four men;
When he came into battle
He slew as would a hundred . . . . . .

The powers here enumerated are powers of mighty men, but the earliest Arthurian tale, *Culhwch and Olwen,* in listing the entire roster of Arthur's knights in their Welsh versions, expands on the mythological attributes of these warriors:

Cei had this peculiarity, nine nights and nine days his breath lasted under water, nine nights and nine days would he be without sleep. A wound from Cei's sword no physician might heal. A wondrous gift had Cei: when it pleased him he would be as tall as the tallest tree in the forest. Another peculiarity had he: when the rain was heaviest, a handbreadth before his hand and another behind his hand what would be in his hand would be dry, by reason of the greatness of his heat; and when the cold was hardest on his comrades, that would be to them kindling to light a fire.

Arthur called on Bedwyr, who never shrank from an enterprise upon which Cei was bound. It was thus with Bedwyr, that none was so handsome as he in this Island, save Arthur and Drych son of Cibddar, and this too, that though he was one-handed no three warriors drew blood in the same field faster than he. Another strange quality was his; one thrust would there be of his spear, and nine counter-thrusts.

This tale tells of Arthur's cooperation in the winning of Olwen, daughter of Chief Giant Ysbaddaden, to be Culhwch's bride. Much of it concerns a boar hunt that takes the pursuers clear across Wales and Somerset, Devon and Cornwall; when it was over, "Arthur went thence to Celli Wig in Cornwall, to bathe himself and rid him of his weariness."

Celliwig has been identified with two of the hill forts that dominate the trade route across Cornwall from Padstow to Fowey, one near Bodmin and one in Egloshayle parish. A Welsh history published in 1716 names the place as one of

> Arthur's Three Principal Courts:
> Caer y Gamlas (Camelot in Somerset?)
> Gelliwig
> Caerlleon ar Wysg.

In other triads, Arthur is one of the Three Frivolous Bards, one of the Three Red Ravagers; the perpetrator, in his exchanges with Modred, of one of the Three Unrestrained Ravagings of the Island of Britain. It is his participation in an attempted theft that first links his name with Tristan's. Tristan is keeping an eye on the swine of King Mark while the swineherd goes with a message to Iseult; Mark, Arthur, Kay and Bedivere attempt a raid: "but they did not succeed in getting so much as one pigling—neither by force, nor by deception, nor by stealth."

Most triads about Tristan accord better with the later romances: he is one of the Three Lovers of the Island of Britain, and his devotion leads the list of the "Three Surpassing Bonds of Enduring Love

107

which Three Men formerly in the time of Arthur cast upon the Three Fairest, most Lovable, and most Talked-of Maidens who were in the Island of Britain at that time."

Originally, the romance of Tristan and Iseult and the Arthurian cycle were separate groups of stories, but under the magnetism of the latter Tristan became Arthur's nephew.

The placement of the stories of King Mark and Tristan partly in Cornwall and partly in Brittany has historical and geographic support. Legend designates Castle Dore, the Iron Age hill fort above the port of Fowey in Cornwall, as King Mark's military stronghold, and Lancien as his nearby court—the village of Lantyan lies down the hill just north of the castle. There are harbors on either side of the narrow peninsula topped by this rampart-ringed knoll; it monitors the southern end of the trade route across Cornwall from Padstow.

Over this route, in the classical period, gold mined in southern Ireland moved to the Mediterranean; over it, in the Dark Age, Irish saints came to evangelize western Britain and Brittany. The church at Golant, below and east of Castle Dore, is dedicated to St. Samson, who ministered there before crossing to become archbishop of Dol in Brittany—all seven of Brittany's ancient bishoprics had Celtic monks from Britain as their patron-founders.

A 9th century Breton life of a 6th century Celtic saint, Paul Aurelian, who trained in Wales, lived in Cornwall and died in Brittany, reveals that King Mark was also known as Cunomorus: "fama eius regis Marco pervolat ad aures, quem alio nomine Quonomorium vocant." In the form of Kynvawr, this version of his name also occurs in Welsh pedigrees of the ruling line of Devon and Cornwall.

In the eyes of most churchmen, he was as rude a character as they held Arthur to be, and his conduct even more reprehensible; several ecclesiastical biographers make invidious mention of him as ruler of southwest Britain and of Breton Dumnonia. Gregory of Tours reports that the excesses Mark committed in Brittany, first as regent and then as usurper, so outraged several saints that they went to Paris and sought aid from the Frankish king, Childebert I. Their petition was sympathetically received: taking the field Childebert defeated and killed Mark in December, 560.

Not only the written record but a stone inscription commemorates Mark and Tristan. At a crossroads near Castle Dore, moved from a previous location near Menabilly in relatively recent times, stands a tall plinth with a tau cross. Its much-eroded lettering can be deciphered in certain lights: Hic jacet Drustanus Cunomori filius. In the romances, Tristan appears as Mark's nephew rather than his son, but there seems no doubt that both were historic characters, and the variety of firm evidence regarding them is certainly greater than in the case of any other heroes of the Arthurian cycle.

Another historic contemporary, who like Tristan was originally the hero of an independent cycle of tales but whose story was later merged with Arthur's, was Geraint of the Devon-Cornwall peninsula.

The fusion had taken place by the time the storytellers of the *Mabinogion* presented him as Geraint Son of Erbin in a tale that begins: "It was Arthur's custom to hold court at Caer Llion on Usk, and he held it continually for seven Easters and five Christmasses. And once upon a time he held court there at Whitsuntide; for Caer Llion was the most accessible place in his dominions, by sea and by land." It was to this court that Geraint brought the maiden Enid to be bestowed on him by Arthur, and from it he set out, escorted by a goodly company of Arthur's men, to safeguard the lands of his aging father, Erbin in Dumnonia. In later years, the testing of Enid that took place in the course of their adventures, and her constancy became a favorite romantic theme on the Continent as well as among the Celts.

THE REALMS OF ARTHUR

As to the historic Geraint, one of the longer Welsh poems is a lament extolling him and his horses, written after his death in a battle led by Arthur.

> *Before Geraint*   *the enemy's scourge*
> *I saw white horses*   *tensed, red*
> *After the war cry*   *bitter the grave . . . . .*
>
> *In Llongborth*   *I saw the clash of swords*
> *Men in terror,*   *bloody heads,*
> *Before Geraint the Great,*   *his father's son. . . .*
>
> *In Llongborth*   *I saw Arthur,*
> *Heroes*   *who cut with steel,*
> *The Emperor*   *ruler of our labour.*
>
> *In Llongborth*   *Geraint was slain*
> *Heroes*   *of the land of Dyfnaint*
> *And before they were slain*   *they slew .*
>
> *Under the thigh of Geraint*   *swift chargers*
> *Long their legs*   *wheat their fodder*
> *Red, swooping*   *like milk-white eagles . . . . .*
>
> *When Geraint was born*   *Heaven's gate stood open*
> *Christ granted*   *all our prayer*
> *Lovely to behold*   *the glory of Britain.*

Some writers believe Llongborth to be Langport in Somerset between Glastonbury and Taunton, where the Saxons triumphed in the 9th century. But since the name is taken to mean 'port of the warships', the battle should probably be placed on the south coast at Portchester. The *Anglo-Saxon Chronicle* supports such attribution: under the year 501 it reports: "In this year, Port and his two sons Bieda and Maegla, came to Britain at the place which is called Portsmouth, and there they killed a young British man of very high rank." Above Llangollen in Wales, the hill opposite Dinas Bran bears Geraint's name.

The triad on the Three Great Queens of Arthur's Court introduces Guenevere:

> "Gwennhwyfar daughter of (Cywryd) Gwent,
> and Gwenhwyfar daughter of (Gwythyr) son of Griediawl,
> and Gwenhyfar daughter of (G)ogfran the Giant."

The last Guenevere was Arthur's queen. Her giant father, whose home, Caer Gogyrfan, was the hill fort at Knucklas above Knighton on the River Teme, had to be forcibly persuaded of the match.

Most accounts follow that which says of her that "Arthur cherished her dearly, for his love was wonderfully set upon the damsel, yet never had they a child together, nor betwixt them might get an heir," but two sons of Arthur figure in tale and triad. The triads name one, Llacheu, along with Gawain as both fearless and well-endowed; as Lohot, he appears in the French romance *Perlesvaus,* where extensive episodes tell how he kills a giant and is slain by Kay, and how Arthur discovers Kay's concealment of the killing.

The grave of another son of Arthur is mentioned among the twenty *Marvels of Britain* appended to Nennius' manuscript. Two marvels relate to Arthur; this one concerns a sepulcher by a well named Licat Anir. The author of the 'marvels' declares that he himself has verified the fact that this tomb never measures the same, and says: "The name of the man who is buried in the tumulus was called so, Anir. He was the son of Arthur the soldier, and he killed him in the same place and buried him."

The "eye-spring of the Anir" still bubbles at Gamber Head on the edge of a farm northwest of Llanwarne and west of the Wye in Herefordshire; geologists believe that the spring water stirring the sand in year-round constant flow comes from many miles away, either from the Black Hills to the west, or the Malvern Hills on the plain of the Severn.

The other Arthurian 'marvel' concerns his dog, Cabal, who left his print on a pile of stone;

> When he hunted the boar Troynt, Cabal, who was the dog of Arthur the soldier, impressed his footprint on the stone and Arthur afterwards collected a pile of stones under the stone, whereon was the footprint of his dog, and it is called Carn Cabal. And men come and carry the stone in their hands for the space of a day and a night, and on the morrow it is found upon its pile.

Cabal is a curious name for a dog, since 'caballus' is Latin for horse. But Cabal's Cairn still wrinkles the skyline of a 1500 foot ridge in the extreme north of Brecknockshire. Starting from the village of Elan in the valley of the Elan River southwest of Rhyader, a country road climbs through sun-flecked bracken in a forest of ancient oaks, then levels through upland fields. Today's name of the ridge—now

113

spelled Corngafallt—recognizes its past; strangers who climb to the top frequently gather the loose stones there into a pile again.

Wales and the West Country subscribed firmly to the belief in Arthur as rex quondam, rex futurus, the king who did not die but sleeps and will come again to lead his people.

Herman of Tournai visited England in 1113 on a fund-raising trip to rebuild the burned cathedral of Laon. On the road from Exeter to Bodmin, he was shown Arthur's Chair and Arthur's Oven; at Bodmin, a bloody-nosed brawl broke out when a pugnacious Cornishman attempted to convince one of the French party that Arthur was still alive—"exactly," says Herman, "in the same way as the inhabitants of Britain (Brittany) dispute with the French over Arthur."

True, at the top of a road that slants almost vertically up to the ridge above Dorstone in Herefordshire, a majestic site surveying the valley of the Dore bears a Neolithic burial chamber known as the Stone of Arthur. But this height is far outnumbered by the many Welsh caves in which he is held to bide his time.

On the flank of Little Doward Hill above the Wye northeast of Monmouth in Herefordshire, high in a concealing beech wood near a quarry, is a large cave known as Arthur's where archaeological investigation has established human occupancy from Paleolithic times into the 5th century A.D. Its recesses penetrate very far into the hill, and could hide a substantial force.

THE REALMS OF ARTHUR

Other caves that bear his name are at Craig-y-Dinas in Glamorganshire, on Snowdon, in Anglesey; from as far away as Sewingshields on the Wall come legends of shepherds who stumbled on such hiding places, entered and saw, and in some cases woke Arthur and his men, fled in fear, and could never find the place again.

A stanza in the Welsh *Song of the Graves* repeats the belief that for him there was no burial:

> *Osvran's son's grave at Camlan,*
> *After many a slaughter,*
> *Bedwyr's grave in Allt Tryvan.*
> *A grave for March, a grave for Gwythur,*
> *A grave for Gwgawn of the ruddy sword,*
> *Not wise (the thought) a grave for Arthur.*

Arthur's expected return to save his people merges his story with Celtic mythology. Earlier, this role was attributed to Bran, a god-hero who possessed a magic cauldron of plenty to supply the needs of all. Dinas Bran, the thousand foot mountain above Llangollen, was his stronghold—his size was such that no house could hold him and he waded across the Irish Sea. Atop that mountain, inside the Iron Age hill fort's ramparts, are the ruins of a castle begun by Gruffydd Maelor, late 12th century ruler of the kingdom of Powys, and extended by his grandson; conspicuous from all directions, the walls stand in black outline against the sky. Like many others, this hill is known to contain treasure: a harp of gold will be found by a boy followed by a white dog with a silver eye—such dogs can see the wind. To the north of Dinas Bran runs a mammoth ridge of exposed strata so clean-cut that they look like man-made walls; its furthest tip is called Craig Arthur.

After Bran's death his severed head—Celtic mythology abounds in severed heads—fulfilled the function earlier served by his cauldron. Eventually, the head was buried on Tower Hill in London. Its value as a talisman and Arthur's jealousy are affirmed in the triad that re-

counts the Three Fortunate Concealments and the Three Unfortunate
Disclosures:

> The Head of Brân the Blessed, son of Llŷr, which was concealed in the
> White Hill in London, with its face towards France. And as long as it
> was in the position in which it was put there, no Saxon Oppression
> would ever come to this Island;
>
> The second Fortunate Concealment: the Dragons in Dinas Emrys,
> which Lludd son of Beli concealed;
>
> And the third: the Bones of Gwerthefyr the Blessed, in the Chief
> Ports of this Island. And as long as they remained in that concealment,
> no Saxon Oppression would ever come to this Island.
>
> And they were the Three Unfortunate Disclosures when these

were disclosed. And Gwrtheyrn* the Thin disclosed the bones of Gwerthefyr the Blessed for the love of a woman: that was Ronnwen** the pagan woman;

And it was he who disclosed the Dragons;

And Arthur disclosed the Head of Brân the Blessed from the White Hill, because it did not seem right to him that this Island should be defended by the strength of anyone, but by his own.

* Vortigern
** Hengist's daughter Rowena, whom Vortigern married

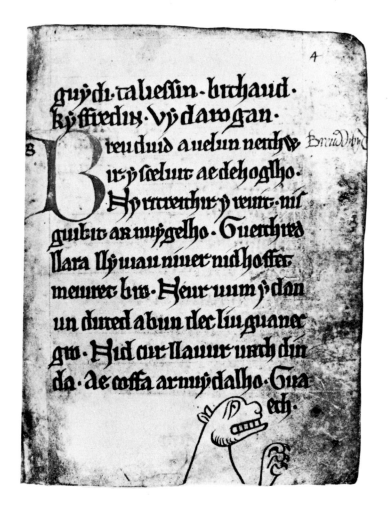

The mythological Arthur also takes voyages in his ship Prydwen to caers of the Otherworld, sometimes this is described as a Tower of Glass, sometimes merely as a Western Island, perhaps Grassholm, off the southwest tip of Wales.

The glimpses of the chief Arthurian characters provided by the triads seem stark indeed when compared with the descriptions in the storytellers' tales. These entertainers belonged to a tradition that could put all winter into three lines:

> *The fish's bed is cold under the ice,*
> *the stag is lean, the reeds are bearded;*
> *the evening is short, trees bend . . . . .*

Their color and fragrance are unrivalled; when Olwen makes her entrance she is a Primavera trailing the blossoms of a Celtic spring:

> She came, with a robe of flame-red silk about her, and around the maiden's neck a torque of red gold, and precious pearls thereon and rubies. Yellower was her head than the flower of the broom, whiter was her flesh than the foam of the wave; whiter were her palms and her fingers than the shoots of the marsh trefoil from amidst the fine gravel of a welling spring. Neither the eye of the mewed hawk, nor the eye of the thrice-mewed falcon, not an eye was there fairer than hers. Whiter were her breasts than the breast of the white swan, redder were her cheeks than the reddest foxgloves. Whoso beheld her would be filled with love of her. Four white trefoils sprang up behind her wherever she went; and for that reason she was called Olwen.

As the storytellers conjured magic, they saw no incongruity in evoking it from the mire of a peasant farm. The *Dream of Rhonabwy* is a tapestry hung in a hut. In the course of a harrying, on a night of storm and rain, while his men slept on "dusty flea-ridden straw-ends, Rhonabwy stretched out on a yellow ox-hide and dreamed a dream." In the dream, Arthur and Owein, like figures in the framing of scenes in a tapestry, play a game of drafts while successive riders arrive with news of an offstage struggle between Arthur's knights and Owein's ravens. The interest is in the panoply of the knights; the eyes of audiences seated on flea-ridden straw-ends would widen at descriptions such as this:

> they could hear a rider coming towards them upon a dapple-grey horse. An exceeding strange colour was upon his horse, dapple-grey and his right leg bright red, and from the top of his legs to the middle of his hoof-horn bright yellow; the rider and his horse arrayed in heavy foreign armour. The housing of his horse from his front saddle-bow upwards pure red sendal, and from the saddlebow downwards pure yellow sendal. A huge gold-hilted one-edged sword on the youth's thigh, and a new bright green scabbard to it, and a tip to the scabbard of laton of Spain; his sword belt of black fleecy cordwain, and gilt crossbars upon it, and a clasp of ivory thereon. And a pure black tongue to the clasp. A gold helm upon the rider's head, and precious stones of great virtue therein, and on top of the helm the image of a yellow-red leopard with two bright red stones in its head, so that it was dreadful for a warrior, however stout his heart might be, to look on the face of the leopard, let alone on the face of the rider. A long heavy green-shafted spear in his hand, and from its hand-grip upwards bright red; the head of the spear red with the blood of the ravens and their plumage.

The final paragraph of the tale as written down states

> the reason why no one, neither bard nor storyteller, knows the Dream without a book—by reason of the number of colours that were on the horses, and all that variety of rare colours both on the arms and their trappings, and on the precious mantles, and the magic stones.

Ensuing generations of bards and storytellers spread such tales of Arthur and his companions far and wide on the Continent, introducing them to areas where the way of life of the Roman years had continued in an enduringly Latinized society and where the language of the Romans had become the root of contemporary speech. One historian has remarked that the people who spoke Latin in early

Britain bore about the same relation to the general population as the people who spoke French in the Russia of Dostoevsky.

Upper-class Romano-Britons of villa and town spoke Latin as a sign of status, and some of the more humble folk—suppliers, retainers, slaves—who were closely associated with them picked up a word or two. The scrawlers of graffiti on the shards found at Silchester knew such characteristic graffiti-scrawler words as 'puella'—girl and 'perfidus'—unfaithful. British administrators of the tribal capitals transacted civic business and erected civic monuments using the language of Rome. The 6th century Celtic saints who evangelized in Britain and Brittany continued the tradition of church Latin.

But except for these special groups, the average Briton was not Romanized; in Kent, where Roman influence came soonest, Saxon impact came soonest, too. Thereafter, the Latin language rapidly disappeared.

Across the Channel, by contrast, learned churchmen like Gregory of Tours could not only follow the Mass but use Latin proficiently as a tool of thought. As Latin was adapted in a new vernacular, French became the common tongue among all strata of society. By the opening of the medieval period, the upper classes were served by secular and professional literary men familiar with classical literature.

To these writers, ever eager for new story material, the fables of the Britons came at the right time. One of the Celtic transmitters has even left a name: a Welshman called Bleheris was at the court of Poitou in the 1130's, during the girlhood of Eleanor of Aquitaine. Continental poets specifically cite him as their source: a late 12th century description of Wales refers to him as "famosus ille fabulator."

Yet by the mid-12th century, Celtic grist for French mills was obtained from other than Breton sources. King Henry II, himself a son of Anjou, and Queen Eleanor, herself a daughter of Aquitaine, had their court in London, but also ruled Western France from the Pyrenees to the borders of modern Belgium. French writers found it natural to accompany their French patrons to Britain, and there they heard the stories themselves at first hand.

121

Chrétien de Troyes, one of the most prolific of French romancers, is thought almost certainly to have crossed the Channel, partly because of the geographic knowledge exhibited in his *Cliges*—an Arthurian tourney at Galinguefort corresponds to the meeting of Henry II and his barons at Wallingford—and partly because of his equally accurate description of seasickness.

At the same time, noble patrons made available to their preferred poets the manuscripts that had recently begun to multiply: it became fashionable for authors on both sides of the Channel to claim to have been "shown a book." The device invested their work with antecedent authority, however spurious, and left them free to "tell the tale as it was told to me."

V

THE
ARTHUR
OF
CHRONICLE

D OWN THE YEARS TO THE 12TH CENTURY, GILDAS, Bede and Nennius are the historians of the Arthurian epic, and Celtic literature its elaborator. Then, some time during 1136–38, Geoffrey of Monmouth finished his *History of the Kings of Britain,* an account blending magic, majesty, and pseudo-history, and created a new realm for the Arthur of chronicle.

The Arthurian story was not the same thereafter. The early historians had bequeathed scraps of fact; from imaginative memories, the Welsh singers and storytellers had created Celtic landscapes with figures. Geoffrey, who came from Monmouthshire on the border between England and Wales, drew alike on the data of the former and

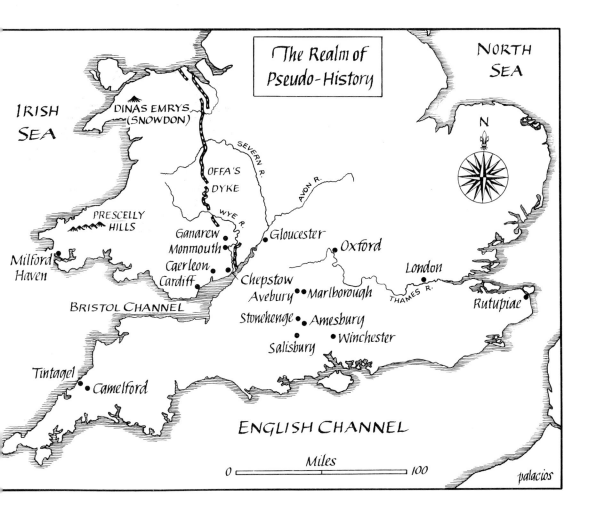

the marvels of the latter. Writing for the Anglo-Norman establishment, he combined his sources in an ordered sequence of kingly succession. It enhanced the royal line founded by William the Conqueror, and set the form taken by the Arthurian legend in medieval times.

In the Arthurian episodes that form a very large part of his text, Arthur becomes king of England. Where a Welsh triad names as his courts three places in the western mountain zone, Geoffrey's Arthur holds high festival in Winchester and London as well as Carlisle and Caerleon. After his uncle Ambrosius clears the Anglo-Saxons from the east coast as far as York, Arthur consolidates this territory and restores

125

the Scottish kingdoms from Lothian to Moray. Subsequent overseas conquests secure for him the primacy among European monarchs.

But Geoffrey's chronicle by no means moves forward in a straight-line account of human affairs. The magic of Merlin, who appears as a boy in the time of Vortigern, waxes in the reign of Uther Pendragon, Arthur's father. Portents in the sky, dreams before battle, combats with giants, and after Camlann, removal to the other-world Isle of Avalon are part and parcel of the tale. Yet Geoffrey established a sequence of events and a biography of Arthur that had previously been lacking. His book was circulated with alacrity.

By January 1139, a copy of his manuscript was being exhibited in Normandy. In England, a translation from his rather heavy Latin into Anglo-Norman verse was promptly undertaken at the request of the wife of an Anglo-Norman baron in Lincolnshire. By 1155, a further translation, likewise in verse, had been completed by Maistre Wace of Caen, a Jerseyman who spent most of his life in France.

Noble connoisseurs on both sides of the Channel busied transcribers and illuminators with orders for copies. A spate of children named Arthur witnessed the warrior's —by now, the king's —new popularity; one of them, the posthumous son of the Duke of Brittany, had one real king, Henry II, for his grandfather, and another, Richard Coeur de Lion, for his uncle. Artusius and Galvanus suddenly recurred as far away as north Italy; Tristan was in vogue over much of Western Europe.

Geoffrey of Monmouth himself signed his name on occasion, 'Geoffrey, son of Arthur'. He was either a native Welshman or one of the many Bretons who returned after the Conquest to the lands that their forebears had left 500 years before. After 1075, the town of Monmouth at the junction of the Monnow and the Wye was in Breton hands, but Geoffrey spent much of his adult life at Oxford, attached to the secular college of St. George's within the castle precinct, founded by the Norman Robert d'Oili in 1074. Between 1129 and 1151 his signature appears a number of times as witness to land titles of nearby ecclesiastical foundations such as Osney, Godstow and Thame; Osney absorbed St. George's in 1149.

But he retained his connection with Wales. After his uncle became bishop of Llandaff, he was made archdeacon there; further ecclesiastical preferment came to him in a nomination to the bishopric of St. Asaph's in Flintshire in 1151. He was consecrated at Lambeth early in 1152, and the next year witnessed the document in which King Stephen recognized Queen Mathilda's son Henry as his successor. But the likelihood of his ever having been installed in his see is marginal; he died in 1155 and during the middle years of the 12th century the rulers of central and northern Wales nodded only faintly in recognition of Anglo-Norman sovereignty.

The territory west of Offa's Dyke was perennially difficult: Anglo-Norman kings encountered the same resistance as Saxon and Roman before them. Along the same frontier where the Romans had set their great legionary fortresses, William the Conqueror appointed three border earls, giving them license to conduct private Norman conquests westward as they were able. Their string of castles followed the old line: the wall of the Roman fort at Cardiff became the frame for a Norman motte. The impression of crushing force conveyed by the Roman camp at Caerleon—even by the single section of its barracks visible today—was repeated in medieval military architecture a few miles northeast where Chepstow Castle keeps watch on the Wye just above its outflow into the Severn Estuary: the Severn bore daily pushes and pulls a twenty-foot tide beside its walls. Further up river, the same lord erected the castle at Monmouth.

Even though Geoffrey rarely lived there, this was his country. When he came to write his *History,* he claimed a Welsh source for it, declaring it to be a translation undertaken after Walter, archdeacon of Oxford, "offer'd me a very ancient Book in the *British* tongue." The claim arouses suspicion: at that time, the Welsh oral tradition was barely beginning to yield to transcription; Gildas, Nennius and Bede were in Latin. Yet at the end of his work Geoffrey warns off his contemporary historians, William of Malmesbury and Henry of Huntingdon, telling them to confine their writings to Saxon rather than British kings:

> I recommend these last to say nothing at all about the kings of the Britons, seeing that they do not have in their possession the book in the British language which Walter, Archdeacon of Oxford, brought from Wales. It is this book which I have been at such pains to translate into Latin in this way, for it was composed with great accuracy about the doings of these princes and in their honour.

128   Scepticism about the authenticity of Geoffrey's work existed from the first: the author of a *Journey Through Wales* near the end of the

century said that a compatriot in Caerleon, who was plagued by evil spirits, became calm when a Gospel according to St. John was placed on his breast, but disturbed when it was replaced by Geoffrey's *History*. A roughly contemporary English judgment was even harsher:

> everything this man wrote about Arthur and his successors, or indeed about his predecessors from Vortigern onwards, was made up, partly by himself and partly by others, either from an inordinate love of lying, or for the sake of pleasing the Britons.

Geoffrey dedicated his book to Robert, King Henry I's illegitimate son who was made Earl of Gloucester in the 1120's. Since, following Henry's death in 1135, this Robert espoused the cause of his half-sister Mathilda against their cousin Stephen in his struggle for the crown, the dedication became something of an embarrassment; one edition substitutes Stephen's name for Robert's. But in the West Country, Robert was unchallenged: besides holding the crossing of the Severn at Gloucester, he had castles further down on both sides at Bristol and Cardiff.

In his dedicatory epistle, Geoffrey explains what led him to write his history:

> Whenever I have chanced to think about the history of the kings of Britain, on those occasions when I have been turning over a great many such matters in my mind, it has seemed a remarkable thing to me that, apart from such mention of them as Gildas and Bede had each made in a brilliant book on the subject, I have not been able to discover anything at all on the kings who lived here before the Incarnation of Christ, or indeed about Arthur and all the others who followed on after the Incarnation. Yet the deeds of these men were such that they deserve to be praised for all time.

In praising the early inhabitants of "Britain, the best of islands," however, he faced a delicate problem. The Normans had conquered the Saxons, and the Saxons had conquered the Britons. How then to make the Britons heroic as the wellspring of the island's sovereignty?

Gildas' strictures on the manner of life of the kings of his day

had been used by the respected Anglo-Saxon monk Alcuin of York to justify Saxon conquest of "the country which God conceded by his free gift to our forefathers." Geoffrey followed his lead: the descendants of the early Britons had rapidly deteriorated:

> Britain is inhabited by five races of people, the Norman-French, the Britons, the Saxons, the Picts and the Scots. Of these the Britons once occupied the land from sea to sea, before the others came. Then the vengeance of God overtook them because of their arrogance and they submitted to the Picts and the Saxons.

A summary of Geoffrey's Arthurian account outlines the thenceforth accepted canon.

His King Constantine corresponds to the Constantinius of Honorius' time; Geoffrey names his three young sons as Constans, who when grown became a monk, Aurelius Ambrosius, and Uther. When Constantine dies, there is dissension as to which of the brothers, the two younger still in their boyhood, shall be crowned. Seizing an opportunity, the Welsh king Vortigern extracts Constans from his monastery, crowns him, causes him to be killed, and usurps. Aurelius Ambrosius and Uther flee to Brittany and the protection of the Armorican king.

Vortigern invites in the Saxons and gives them a number of hides of valuable land in Kent. (A favorite illustration of this passage

shows Hengist about to slaughter an ox; he intends to cut the hide into the narrowest of strips to mark the largest possible perimeter of his new holdings.) Vortigern, already old enough to have grown sons, marries Hengist's daughter Rowena and waxes uxorious. Disgruntled Britons name his son Vortimer king in his stead. Before

Rowena succeeds in having Vortimer poisoned, he pushes back the Saxons in four major battles. Meanwhile, Hengist holds Vortigern prisoner and forces him to give up a series of strategic strongholds before setting him free.

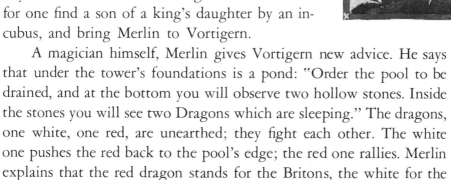

Vortigern flees to Wales and begins to build a strong tower on Dinas Emrys (Snowdon) as his ultimate retreat. Mysteriously, work done by day disappears by night. Vortigern's magicians tell him that to break this spell he must sacrifice a boy without a father. Messengers sent to search for one find a son of a king's daughter by an incubus, and bring Merlin to Vortigern.

A magician himself, Merlin gives Vortigern new advice. He says that under the tower's foundations is a pond: "Order the pool to be drained, and at the bottom you will observe two hollow stones. Inside the stones you will see two Dragons which are sleeping." The dragons, one white, one red, are unearthed; they fight each other. The white one pushes the red back to the pool's edge; the red one rallies. Merlin explains that the red dragon stands for the Britons, the white for the Saxons, and that the end of the red dragon is near. He likewise fore-

tells that Vortigern will be burned alive, and that Aurelius Ambrosius and Uther will succeed to the kingship.

Almost at once, the two princes arrive with a force of 10,000 Armoricans. Ambrosius is anointed king; he pursues Vortigern into Wales and burns his tower with him in it.

(In this passage, Geoffrey's fondness for his own part of Herefordshire causes him to change the location of Vortigern's tower. It was built on Snowdon, but it was burned on a site that must have been familiar from Geoffrey's youth: "the castle of Genoreu." This castle, he says, "was beside the Wye on a hill called Cloartius." A village between Monmouth and Whitchurch is still called Ganarew; above it, an Iron Age fort tops Little Doward Hill—the same hill in whose flank is Arthur's Cave.)

Ambrosius then wins two decisive engagements with the Saxons, cavalry charges gaining the victory; shortly, Octa, son of Hengist, yields York. His enemies subdued, Ambrosius restores London, Winchester and Salisbury. His mind then turns to a war memorial.

To his amazement, Merlin advises him to move the Giant's Dance from Mount Killaraus in Ireland.

'How can such large stones be moved from so far-distant a country?' he asked. 'It is hardly as if Britain itself is lacking in stones big enough for the job!'

'Try not to laugh in a foolish way, your Majesty,' answered Merlin. 'What I am suggesting has nothing ludicrous about it. These stones are connected with certain secret religious rites and they have various properties which are medicinally important.'

Convinced, Ambrosius puts Uther in charge of the removal: watching his men's futile efforts, Merlin

burst out laughing. He placed in position all the gear which he considered necessary and dismantled the stones more easily than you could ever believe. Once he had pulled them down, he had them carried to the ships and stored on board, and they all set sail once more for Britain with joy in their hearts.

To celebrate the erection of Stonehenge, Ambrosius summons all Britain; he is re-crowned on the Mount of Ambrius at Whitsuntide. When shortly thereafter, through the connivance of a son of Vortigern who is king of Ireland, he is poisoned at Winchester, his body is brought for interment to his Sepulcher of Stones.

Archaeological analysis of Stonehenge shows that some of the stones did indeed come from afar, though from Wales rather than Ireland. Of the two concentric circles of monoliths, the large sarsen stones of the outer circle and the outer horseshoe were obtained near Marlborough, where Merlin is said to sleep in the mound inside the grounds of Marlborough School. That is a crowflight distance of some twenty miles. The bluestones of the inner circle and the inner horseshoe came from a far greater distance—all the way from the Prescelly Hills in Pembrokeshire. The altar stone is from near Milford Haven.

Experiments have tested ways of transporting such huge weights: they were probably moved by boat over much of the distance from source to site, then hauled overland; when erected, they may have been hoisted up huge inclined planes, then tilted upright into prepared holes.

133

The surfaces of the Stonehenge monoliths, unlike those of the more extensive monument at nearby Avebury, are dressed. Lintels, secured in place by mortice holes fitted over tenons carved on the uprights, originally topped all of the outer circle—enough remain now to show how the whole once looked. The larger horseshoe inside the circle was formed of similarly constructed trilithons of still greater height—one member of the tallest of these still stands upright, the tenon that held its fallen lintel protruding into the sky.

Popular conviction to the contrary, Stonehenge was not erected by the Druids—it far predates their presence in Britain. There is scientific unanimity in repudiating this origin.

But as to the purpose of the Stone Age people who did build it in successive stages from about 2000 to 1500 B.C. scientists argue violently. Was it designed for celebration of rites connected with the cycle of the agricultural year, or was it a still more sophisticated edifice, an astronomical observatory enabling both calculation and prediction of the movements of sun and moon?

Modern computers have checked the alignments of the stone circles, the inner trilithons, and also the circle of 56 mysterious "Aubrey holes", so known from the antiquary who first investigated them, whose positions are now marked in chalk, forming a periphery of the precinct. The results indicate that the monument could have been used for calculations of the 19-year cycle that was known among classical Greeks as the Great Year. Nineteen solar years and 235 lunations both equal slightly more than 6,939 days; at 19-year intervals, therefore, sun and moon return to the same relationship. This degree of sophistication seems hard to credit to the astronomical observations of a Stone Age people—even though the English climate of their time is known to have afforded clearer as well as warmer weather than it does today. Yet the position of the stones remains to be explained.

Controversy also exists as to whether the prime purpose of the rites at this scene was to celebrate the summer or the winter solstice. Past opinion has favored the summer turning of the sun: on June 21 it rises over the 'heelstone' that time has eroded to the image of a laughing dolphin just outside the Aubrey hole circle and in the path of the processional avenue to the east of the monument. But a currently strong view notes that the December 21 position of the sun centers in the slot that would have been formed by the greatest of the trilithons. The beginning of renewal following the death of the old year seems a more likely basis of solemn celebration than the sunrise of midsummer. If this were the purpose of the major ceremony, the processional approach from the east, comparable to the West

Kennett avenue at Avebury, would have led celebrants into the apses formed by the horseshoes and centering on the great trilithon.

Among unsolved mysteries of the monument is the origin of the double-ax and dagger designs observed on several of the monoliths in recent years—do they imply a connection between the men who built this monument and their contemporary Minoan and Mycenaean movers of mammoth stones in prehistoric Greece?

Geoffrey says that when Ambrosius died at Winchester, there appeared in the sky a ball of fire that took the form of a dragon. Uther had two gold standards made in its likeness, giving one to

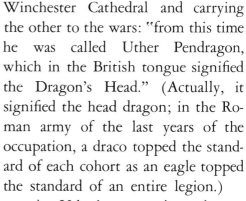

Winchester Cathedral and carrying the other to the wars: "from this time he was called Uther Pendragon, which in the British tongue signified the Dragon's Head." (Actually, it signified the head dragon; in the Roman army of the last years of the occupation, a draco topped the standard of each cohort as an eagle topped the standard of an entire legion.)

At Uther's coronation, the attending chieftains include Gorlois, Duke of Cornwall, and his wife Igerna. Uther is seized with a passion for Igerna; observing it, she and Gorlois leave the court, angering Uther by not asking permission to depart. Anticipating pursuit, Gorlois sets up a decoy. He puts Igerna in Tintagel, one of his two castles in Cornwall, and invites attack at Dimilioc, his other main stronghold. But Merlin changes Uther into the likeness of Gorlois; at Tintagel, he is admitted without question.

Who, indeed, could possibly have suspected anything, once it was thought that Gorlois himself had come? The King spent that night with Ygerna and satisfied his desire by making love with her. He had deceived her by the disguise which he had taken. He had deceived her, too, by the lying things that he said to her, things which he planned with very great skill. . . . She naturally believed all that he said and refused him nothing that he asked. That night she conceived Arthur, the most famous of men, who subsequently won great renown by his outstanding bravery.

While this is going on, Gorlois is conveniently killed. Uther marries Igerna, who in addition to Arthur bears him a daughter Anna.

At the time appropriate to these events, the black crag of Tintagel, protruding into the Cornish sea, was still connected with the mainland by a natural causeway that arched over foaming water as does the present ceiling of the cave where Merlin is said to have waited during Uther's visit. Geoffrey describes it:

> The castle is built high above the sea, which surrounds it on all sides, and there is no other way in except that offered by a narrow isthmus of rock. Three armed soldiers could hold it against you, even if you stood there with the whole kingdom of Britain at your side.

Excavation has shown that in the second half of the fourth century a farmstead was established on this promontory; it was abandoned before the Celtic monk St. Julian and two companions set cells here,

and probably a small church, around the year 500. The outlines of the monastery as later expanded are now exposed. The earliest castle was probably built by Reginald, illegitimate son of Henry I who became Earl of Cornwall and held this territory during the latter part of

Geoffrey's time. The present castle ruins, spread over several levels on both island and landward side, were mainly built by Earl Richard, younger brother of Henry II, in the mid-13th century.

Under Uther, Geoffrey states, the Britons are forced into many retreats; though ill, the king insists on being carried in a horse-litter with his armies until he dies of water from a poisoned spring. His body, like his brother's, is carried to the "monastery of Ambrius, and buried . . . with royal honours at the side of Aurelius Ambrosius, inside the Giants' Ring."

After a conference at Silchester, Arthur, though only fifteen, is crowned; with the support of a very large force from Armorica, the

Britons then meet and defeat the Saxons in the northeast. The victory is of sufficient proportions for the Saxons to agree to go home. But once at sea they turn south and round the island, landing at Totnes, whence they devastate the country across to and up the shore of the Severn Estuary: "Then they proceeded by a forced march to the neighbourhood of Bath and besieged the town."

At the news, Arthur comes to Somerset. At Bath Hill, his forces triumph.

During the peace that follows, he marries Guenevere: "she was descended from a noble Roman family and had been brought up in the

household of Duke Cador. She was the most beautiful woman in the entire island."

In the ensuing years, Arthur becomes conqueror of a large part of the Western world. After a campaign ending in Paris with a single combat between him and Flollo, the Roman emperor's tribune, he returns to Britain and holds court in Caerleon at Pentecost.

All chivalry is summoned. Ceremonies in the churches, feasts, and games follow each other: "The knights planned an imitation battle and competed together on horseback, while their womenfolk watched from the top of the city walls and aroused them to passionate excitement by their flirtatious behavior."

But the joyful interlude is interrupted by envoys from Lucius Hiberius, procurator of Rome, demanding resumption of the ancient tribute. Arthur refuses; the two sides prepare for war. Leaving Modred and Guenevere in charge in Britain, Arthur embarks for France. On shipboard, he dreams of a fight in the sky between a bear and a dragon; the dragon burns the bear with its fiery breath and flings the scorched body to the ground. His advisers assure him that he is the dragon: "Arthur, however, was sure that it all meant something different."

141

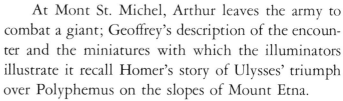

At Mont St. Michel, Arthur leaves the army to combat a giant; Geoffrey's description of the encounter and the miniatures with which the illuminators illustrate it recall Homer's story of Ulysses' triumph over Polyphemus on the slopes of Mount Etna.

When Arthur's forces meet the Romans, Lucius is killed and Arthur commences a march on Rome. As he crosses the Alps, a messenger recalls him to Britain with news of Modred's treachery.

Turning back, he lands at Rutupi and engages Modred. He forces him to retreat, but Gawain is killed in the battle. At York, Guenevere hears of the landing; she goes to Caerleon and takes the veil.

Modred's next stand is at Winchester, where

Arthur gives battle after three days and forces a further retreat.

The last battle is in Cornwall on the river Cambula; there, at the end of an all-day slaughter, Arthur meets and kills Modred in single combat. But "Arthur himself, our renowned king, was mortally wounded and was carried off to the Isle of Avalon, so that his wounds might be attended to. He handed the crown of Britain over to his cousin Constantine, the son of Cador Duke of Cornwall: this in the year 542 after our Lord's Incarnation."

Thus Geoffrey established both a complete biography of Arthur and a sequence of Arthurian history. Continental successors added details, but maintained the substance of his story. As it was translated and adapted, place-names

vary from manuscript to manuscript; while Geoffrey puts the first engagement between Arthur and Modred where the Claudian army landed, others give Sandwich, Dover, Romney or Barham Down elsewhere in Kent. Similarly, the trajectory of the running fight across southern England from Kent to Cornwall crosses the island at different points.

One alternate version has Guenevere become a nun at Amesbury rather than at Caerleon. In 980 the Saxon Queen Elfrida did found a convent at Amesbury, in expiation of the murder of her stepson, Edward the Martyr; the base of one of its columns can still be identified in the present Church of St. Mary and St. Melor.

Only a few miles away is St. Andrew's Church at Nether Wallop. In the floor of its central aisle is the only portrait brass of an abbess known in England; it marks the grave of Maria Gore, who ruled the Amesbury convent and died in 1436.

Her peaceful figure might have served as model for illuminators showing scenes of the reception into penitence of Queen Guenevere:

When Queen Guinevere, the King's wife, knew that all had come to ruin, she went away with five ladies to Amesbury to become a nun. There she lived a holy life, weeping and waking in prayers. Never afterwards could she be happy; there she wore white and black clothes.

PROFESSIONAL TOUCHES

In France, the literary professionals who recast the Arthurian epic were direct heirs of classical antiquity. Horace's *Odes* and Ovid's *Metamorphoses* were their handbooks, secular subjects their preference, especially those treating of love. Under them, the realm of Arthur became a Never-Never Land.

These writers had a special audience, the great ladies of whom Eleanor of Aquitaine and her daughter Marie de Champagne were only the foremost. Geoffrey of Monmouth's *History* had been written with an eye to the interests of the Anglo-Norman kings; the French romancers were the queens' men.

Their manuscripts stimulated the reverie of illustrious chatelaines, perhaps chastity-girdled by Crusading husbands, certainly harassed by the treachery and the royal whim, the sickness and the slaughter of daily real life.

The difference is considerable between the medieval dream castle and the modern dream kitchen, between a noble lady and a bourgeoise housewife, but the romances bear comparison with today's soap opera:

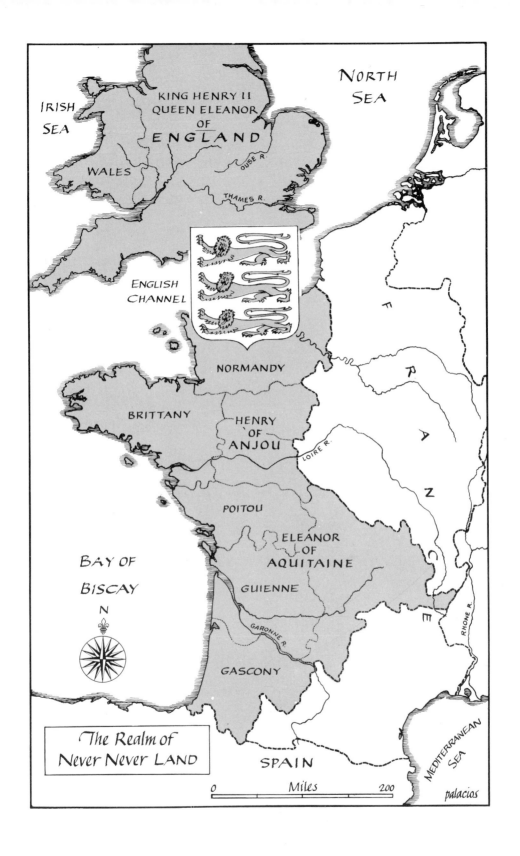

IRISH SEA

WALES

KING HENRY II
QUEEN ELEANOR
OF
ENGLAND

OUSE R.

THAMES R.

NORTH SEA

ENGLISH CHANNEL

NORMANDY

BRITTANY

HENRY
OF
ANJOU

LOIRE R.

F
R
A
N
C
E

POITOU

ELEANOR
OF
AQUITAINE

BAY OF

BISCAY

N

GUIENNE

GARONNE R.

RHONE R.

GASCONY

MEDITERRANEAN SEA

The Realm of
Never Never LAND

SPAIN

0   Miles   200

palacios

when damsels in distress suffer for succor, a glamorous champion comes. Soon, the scarf of the neglected or wronged female flutters as a love token on the crest of a questing knight. Formula fiction multiplies easily.

Under the influence of powerful chatelaines, the battle of the sexes became a combat under elegant rules consonant with the clarity and symmetry of the Gallic mind. Selection of a suitable nuance for a phrase, choice of a response to an artful question, acceptably covert affirmations of passion converted courtly conversation into a sophisticated game. The ladies loved it, and such connoisseurs as Philip of Alsace, Henry II's cousin and Count of Flanders at the same time that Marie was Countess of Champagne, likewise encouraged writers of romance—it was for him that Chrétien de Troyes wrote the first tale of the Grail.

Then and today, to anyone turning illumined pages, reality seems well forgotten as miniatures mirror hunt and hall, stormings of castles and meetings with hermits in forest cells, feasts and quests and tournaments.

Close the book quickly, though, lest reality intrude again. Among the most magnificent of medieval manuscripts is the early 14th century masterpiece, a *Quest* and a *Lancelot,* now known in the British Museum as Royal XIV E III. Its text is surrounded by illumined

margins; its capital letters are miniatures in themselves; its miniatures display the fine work of northern France. Medieval art never surpassed this repository of castle day-dreams. Here, on the first folio inside the massive tooled leather binding, is an owner's signature. To read it is to shiver: the hand that wrote the name was the hand of the learned young woman whom Tudor politics sent to the scaffold for beheading at sixteen—the Lady Jane Grey.

As portrayed by the medieval writers, Arthur and his knights become medieval men. The characters of the romances wear dress and bear devices contemporary with their readers. When Geoffrey of Monmouth armed Arthur for the Battle of Badon, it was in

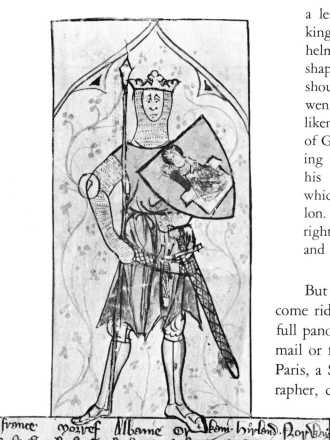

a leather jerkin worthy of so great a king. On his head he placed a gold helmet, with a crest carved in the shape of a dragon; and across his shoulders a circular shield called Pridwen, on which there was painted a likeness of the Blessed Mary, Mother of God, which forced him to be thinking perpetually of her. He girded on his peerless sword, called Caliburn, which was forged in the Isle of Avalon. A spear called Ron graced his right hand: long, broad in the blade and thirsty for slaughter.

But when the romancers' knights come riding, they are decked out in the full panoply of chivalry. They wear steel mail or fully fashioned armor; Matthew Paris, a St. Albans monk and historiographer, compiled the first roster of Arthurian blazons in 1252, and a long succession of such books followed thereafter.

Arthur's first device, as in Geoffrey's description, was taken from Nennius. Actually, this monk said that he "carried the image of the Virgin on his shoulders", but he is regarded as having confused the Welsh word 'ysgwydd' meaning 'shoulder' and 'ysgwyd' meaning 'shield'. By mid-13th century, however, Arthur's usual blazon consists of three crowns, *argent in pale on azure* (silver on blue, arranged vertically) but sometimes *or on gules* (gold on red) arranged two and one; in late medieval days the number of crowns is raised to thirteen.

His three gold crowns on red can be seen in Gloucester Cathedral, on the tomb of Robert Curthose. This Robert was William the Conqueror's eldest son; disinherited and dispossessed after quarreling with his father over lands in France, he spent long years in custody in the west of England. He was known as Robert Curthose because he wore chain mail whose stockings came only to his knees; in the Gloucester choir, a late 12th century painted effigy of him, curthose and all, lies on a 15th century funerary chest whose panels bear painted blazons. These include three real and a number of imaginary devices, Arthur's among the latter. William of Malmesbury complained that this Robert "showered infinite wealth into the laps of mimes and worthless fellows"; perhaps he also listened to storytellers of the once and future king.

Like Arthur's, Lancelot's blazon also varies: sometimes it is a white shield with one, or on occasion three, dark red bands; in one manuscript his shield and horse-trapping bear a heart.

Gawain's virtues are signified by a pentangle; Galahad's, by a red cross

on white or gold. Tristan's lion appears against different colored back-
grounds; it is rampant on the Chertsey tiles. In Germany, his animal
is a boar.

The lists of blazons are almost uniformly attached to treatises
on tourneys. The roughness of the old style of jousting made a ceremonial encounter difficult to distinguish from a battle—because of
its dangers, Henry III forbade a tourney in England in 1235. But the
mid-13th century introduced gentler practice that the title of a mid-
15th century treatise, *La forme quon tenoit des tournoys et assemblees au
temps du roy uterpendragon et du roy artus,* shows to have been credited
to Arthur's court.

Soon, Continental nobility amused itself with Arthurian pag-
eants. Ulrich von Lichtenstein staged an 'Artusfahrt' in 1240, in which
he impersonated Arthur, and his companions other knights; at Ham-
sur-Somme, in 1278, ceremonies centered on a lady acting the part
of Guenevere. Fifteenth century tableaux included a tourney held by
Charles V's grandson, René of Anjou, with background scenery representing Lancelot's castle, Joyous Gard.

French love of precision led Continental writers to endow
Arthur's warriors with new appurtenances as well as with new
panoply. The sword in the stone became the test of Arthur's royal
right. In order that no knight might boast of sitting higher than his
peers, the first translator of Geoffrey of Monmouth introduced the
Round Table:

Por les nobles barons qu'il ot
Dont cascuns mieldre estre quidot. . . .
Fist Artus la Roonde Table,
Dont Breton dient mainte fable.
Illo seoient li vassal
Tuit chievalment et tot ingal. . . .
Nus d'als ne se pooient vanter
Qu'il seist plus halt de son per.

This addition was greatly welcomed in England: celebrations of Mensa Rotunda took place at Wallingford in 1252 and Kenilworth Castle in 1279. In 1344, Edward III presided over a three-day tournament at Windsor and contemplated reviving the Arthurian companionship through the foundation of an order with a membership of three hundred knights. In a new round meeting-hall, two hundred feet in diameter, a feast was held in 1345. But war with France interrupted his plans; three years later, after he discovered that Philip of Valois had already formed a Round Table fellowship, he established the Order of the Garter, with St. George as its patron saint, instead.

A surviving Round Table, eighteen feet in diameter, now hangs on a wall of the Great Hall in Winchester Castle—in a *Chronicle* written 1457–64, the antiquary John Hardyng assumes it to be Arthur's own. In the pattern painted on its surface, lines radiate out from a central white and red Tudor rose; around the circumference, places for twenty-four knights, with that of Arthur at the upper edge and the Siege Perilous on his left, are inscribed with their names. The design

153

probably dates from the crowning of Henry VII, the first Tudor, in 1485—Caxton, who printed Malory's *Morte Darthur* that year, mentions it in his introduction. In 1486, Henry gave his first-born son Arthur's name.

French appreciation of symmetry is evident in lists of Nine Worthies, in which Arthur appears as one of three great Christians. He can be seen in tapestry at the Cloisters in New York, and in the framing of the scenes from the *Book of Revelation* at Angers. In stained glass, he is shown in the windows of St. Mary's Hall, Coventry, and All Souls Chapel, Oxford. In the castle of La Manta in the Italian Piedmont, a painting of about 1430 portrays Nine Worthies and Nine Worthy Women, with the patron and his wife as Hector and Penthesilea; in Italo-French, it designates Arthur:

> I was king of Britain, Scotland, and England. Five hundred kings I conquered, who held their lands from me. I have slain seven great giants in the midst of their land. I went on to conquer still another on Mont St. Michel. I saw the Holy Grail. Then Modred made war on me, who slew me five hundred years after God came to earth.

In addition to these professional touches, the French literateurs

likewise made substantial changes in the Arthurian plots. For their purposes, the Tristan story was perfect as it came from Britain—Tristan, sent by King Mark to fetch Iseult from Ireland; Iseult, married to Mark but pledged to Tristan in fated and undying love after her serving woman, on their way back from Ireland, unwittingly gave them to drink a potion intended for her wedding night; Tristan's quests; his loveless marriage with that other Iseult of Brittany; the voyage of his retainer to fetch Iseult of Ireland when Tristan lies dying, instructed to break out white sails instead of black if she is on board when he returns; the lie told by Iseult of Brittany about their color; the lovers' tragic deaths.

The story of their romance spread from end to end of the Continent. About 1150 the French poet Béroul produced one version; about twenty years later, the Anglo-Norman Thomas completed another. German accounts began early in the 13th century: Gottfried von Strassburg's unfinished work was completed after his death by Heinrich von Freiburg and Ulrich von Tuerheim. The panels of a German tapestry dating from 1370, now in the Victoria and Albert Museum, show Tristan killing a dragon whose severed head a servant then displays to King Mark.

Tristan and Iseult's tryst beneath the tree in the palace garden, spied on by Mark from its upper branches, became a favorite subject for the carvings on 14th century French ivory caskets, with Iseult suddenly seeing the inverted reflection of Mark's face in the pool at her feet.

The entire tale is stitched into a pair of Sicilian bed-quilts, one of which is now in the Victoria and Albert Museum and one in the Bargello in Florence; they are thought to have been made for a wedding in Florence in 1395.

But the main body of Arthurian legend was less suitable for presentation as romance. The writers who adapted it required a

Victoria and Albert Museum. Crown Copyright.

slightly different cast of characters. Accordingly, new persons were invented and old attributes modified.

Arthur becomes a father-figure. He presides over his courts, holds high festival at Christmas, Easter, Whitsun and Pentecost, watches tournaments, but during his reign it is his knights who depart on

camalot   la regine & lanc.

quests and experience adventures. Only at his death is he again the central actor in the piece.

At the same time, a new knight is needed to be first among equals at Arthur's court.

In the Celtic legend, that knight had been Gawain. But Gawain was of limited use to the romancers because this hero was chaste. While he remains a foremost champion, a newcomer to Arthur's court, Lancelot, replaces him as chief knight; this champion is also an incomparable lover.

(Chastity could be laudable: *The Lay of the Horn,* written soon after 1150 by the Anglo-Norman Robert Biket, tells how a youth rode into Arthur's Ascensiontide court at Caerleon with a richly-wrought horn. He declared it would spill on any knight whose wife had been unfaithful to him even in thought. All present, including Arthur, try it and are spilled on except Caradoc, who drinks it down and receives Cirencester as a prize. Biket affirms that the horn may still be seen there.)

The initial appearance of Lancelot's name is in a list of Arthur's knights in Chrétien de Troyes' *Erec,* written about 1168 and soon transmitted to Germany through the work of Hartmann von Aue. Four years later, he becomes Guenevere's lover in Chrétien's *Chevalier de la Charette;* this development too was promptly conveyed to German readers in the *Lanzelet* of Ulrich von Zatzikoven:

King Meleagant has abducted Guenevere. Lancelot pursues, demeaning his knightly dignity by riding in a cart after the loss of his horse. Only two means of access lead to Meleagant's water-surrounded castle: an underwater bridge, and one formed by a sword with its edge turned upward. Lancelot crosses the sword-bridge, fights Meleagant, delivers Guenevere. She reproves him for having even momentarily hesitated to ride in the cart. He attempts suicide. She forgives all. They pass a night together. In reaching her room, Lancelot bloodies his hands wrenching bars from a window. The blood on the sheets implicates the queen and Sir Kay, who, severely wounded, is sleeping in an anteroom. Lancelot offers to prove Guenevere's innocence in

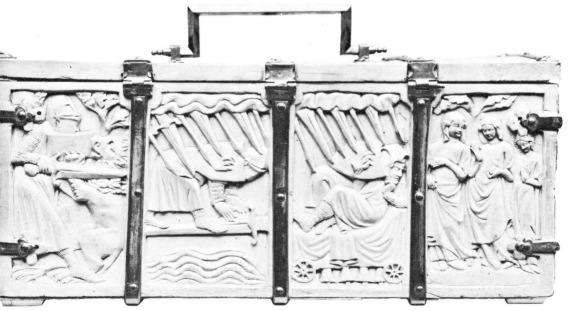

Victoria and Albert Museum. Crown Copyright.

combat with Meleagant; after further episodes, he eventually slays him.

The devotion of Lancelot to Guenevere followed the courtly rules: it was extra-marital, but single-minded. The only instance when it was infringed, Lancelot's begetting of Galahad upon Elaine, daughter of King Pelles, was, like Arthur's incestuous siring of Modred, due to mistaken identity fostered by an enchantress. (The other Elaine, of Astolat, died of unrequited love for the perfect knight.)

The illicit character of courtly love made the French church unfriendly to the romances. At a time just after the real love of the learned Eloise and the theologian Abelard had provided an absorbing ecclesiastical scandal, the increasingly frequent commissioning of illumined copies of such works as the *Lancelot du Lac* now in New York's Morgan Library must have incited the monks engaged in the work to distracting and surreptitious talk during free hours in the cloister—one of the most charming miniatures in this manuscript shows Lancelot and Guenevere's first kiss. The appearance in ecclesiastical buildings of portrayals of secular stories—the Tristan tale on the Abbey tiles at Chertsey, the misericords showing Gawain's horse crushed by a portcullis in English chapels and cathedrals, the capital of the nave pillar in St. Pierre's at Caen, two of whose faces show Lancelot on the Sword Bridge and Gawain on the Perilous Bed—was specifically denounced by such churchmen as Bernard of Cîteaux, who founded the Cistercian order to revive the austerity from which he thought the Benedictines had fallen away.

But noble lady readers unchastenedly applauded Lancelot's obduracy when, in the *Perlesvaus,* he pauses at a monastery to go to confession. Though the monk tells him his sin is mortal, the knight declares himself to be, on one matter, permanently unrepentant:

'Sir', saith Lancelot, 'This sin will I reveal to you of my lips, but of my heart may I never repent me thereof. I love my Lady, which is the Queen, more than aught else that liveth, and albeit one of the best Kings on live hath her to wife. The affection seemeth me so good and so high that I cannot let go thereof, for, so rooted is it in my heart that thence may it nevermore depart, and the

best knighthood that is in me cometh to me only of her affection.'

In the romances, it is the love of Lancelot and the Queen that destroys Arthurian chivalry. In them, the fighting on the Continent that in Geoffrey's *Chronicle* made Arthur master of Europe is replaced by internecine warfare among members of the Round Table.

The protagonists are Gawain and Lancelot. The tragedy begins when Gawain's brothers, Agravaine and Modred, having observed the lovers, determine to tell Arthur. Sensitive to the divisive consequences of the breach the news would cause, Gawain opposes their intent. But they trap the two together in circumstances Arthur cannot ignore. Lancelot kills Agravaine in combat, and cuts down Gawain's two other brothers, Gareth and Gaheris, unarmed. He escapes.

At Winchester, the guilty queen is condemned to the stake. In a spectacular galloping entrance, Lancelot rescues her from the flames and takes her to his castle, thenceforth called Joyous Gard.

The Pope, appalled by the shattering effect of enmity between Lancelot and Arthur, orders Lancelot to return her and Arthur, then holding court at Carlisle, to receive her and forgive him. The Queen

161

returns, but Gawain, smarting under his brothers' deaths, counsels against forgiving Lancelot, and prevails.

Lancelot leaves to muster forces in France; Arthur follows to make war. Gawain seeks a man-to-man encounter with Lancelot; in two successive engagements, Lancelot inflicts on him close-to-mortal wounds.

Then comes news of Modred's betrayal; Gawain, his last wound still unhealed, accompanies Arthur to England and falls in the first battle. Dying, he accepts responsibility for destroying Arthur's knightly fellowship.

The invention of Lancelot was a major French addition to the substance of the Arthurian cycle. Of equal consequence was the introduction of the Grail story. In it, Christian legend and Christian symbolism overlaid pagan allegories of immemorial age. Myths of the fertility cycle—of the annual king who must die if the earth is to be renewed in spring, of the magic food receptacle that can sustain a whole people—merge with the Eucharist, in which Christians receive symbolic sustenance in the body and blood of the crucified Christ.

The church recoiled from the sacerdotal chivalry to which this theme gave rise, but was powerless to suppress this as well as the more secular romances. Two early chronicles supplied its source. Helinand de Froidmont, under the years 717–19, says:

> at this time a wonderful vision was shown to a certain hermit by an angel—a vision concerning a noble decurion, Joseph, who took down the body of our Lord from the cross, and concerning the bowl or dish in which the Lord supped with his disciples in regard to which a history which is called the Grail has been written down by the same hermit.

162   In the first half of the 9th century, the *Chronicle* of Freculfe, bishop of Lisieux, states that not long after the Crucifixion, the apostle

Philip arrived in France with a group of companions on a mission of evangelization. Among them was Joseph of Arimathea, who brought with him the chalice of the Last Supper. Philip shortly designated twelve of his followers, with Joseph at their head, to preach in Britain. There, King Arviragus gave Joseph an island called Ynis Avalon.

Chrétien de Troyes first used the theme with the knights Percival, Bors and Lancelot departing on a Grail quest, in a story that he did not live to finish; it was completed by other writers. In the early 13th century, the Bavarian knight, Wolfram von Eschenbach, wrote the first German *Parzifal.* In some romances, Joseph himself becomes the Maimed King whose impotence, due to a thigh wound, condemns his land to barrenness until he is healed. The Grail quest takes a succession of knights to his castle, where they

163

see the Grail procession pass. Robert de Boron's *Quête del Saint Graal*
completes the story when Galahad takes his place at the Round Table
in the Siege Perilous, finds his shield in an abbey and his sword in a
block of red marble: "He shall end the wonders of Great Britain and
through him the Maimed King shall be healed."

These were not Christian stories, and in general the church dis-
claimed them. But across the Channel, in Britain's West Country, one
enclave of the church, the monks of Glastonbury Abbey, were finding
the stories of Joseph, the Grail legend, and the passing of Arthur of
very practical utility.

THE GLASTONBURY FABLES

MEDIEVAL GLASTONBURY'S ATTITUDE TO THE ARTHURIAN LEGEND was indeed exceptional.

In the general view of the English as well as the French church, the romances were facile tear-jerkers: the renowned Cistercian monk, Ailred of Rievaulx in Yorkshire, who served for a year as his abbey's novice-master, contrasts the effects of the Arthurian stories and the New Testament on their readers in a dialogue with a troubled candidate for ordination.

The novice said that in his old life he had often wept with rapture over Arthurian stories, but now was experiencing a spiritual aridity; yet he preferred his present austere regime to the days when he had found ambivalent pleasure in devout tears and worldly jests, in the love of Christ and in the companionship of the table. As Ailred helped him probe:

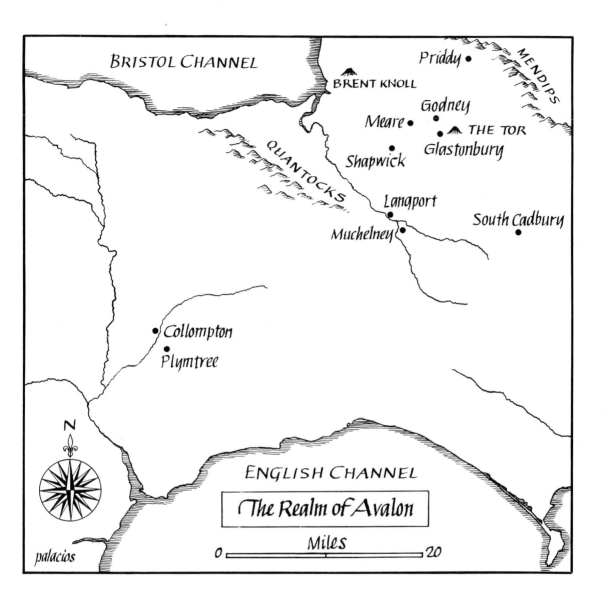

The Realm of Avalon

The conclusion was gradually drawn: to love is one thing, to love with full self-surrender is another and a harder thing. Love without service is like the emotion of a playgoer who weeps at the sight of sufferings which in the street he would pass unmoved. At this point the novice hung his head. He remembered how he, who had been so lightly moved to tears by his love for Christ, had been wont to cry with equal facility over the story of Arthur.

The early Celtic church had treated Arthur as a worldling and as a sinner. Lives of 5th-to-6th century saints enumerate his misconduct and consequent punishment. For instance, when Gwladys, mother of St. Cadoc, eloped with the King of Glamorganshire, with her father in hot pursuit, the couple crested a hill and found Arthur, Kay and Bedivere playing dice. Arthur was seized with a sudden desire to take her for himself; only with effort did his companions dissuade him.

In another story, following a procedure missionaries sometimes used to divine where they should debark in their coracles to evangelize next, the Welsh St. Carannog set his supernatural wooden altar afloat on Bristol Channel. Arthur, whose territory lay opposite in Somerset and Devon, took it ashore. He tried to use it as a table, but repelling the sacrilege, it threw off everything he put on it. When the saint arrived, Arthur gave back the altar, but only on condition that the saint rid the countryside of a dragon. Arthur meant him to slaughter the creature; Carannog gently put his stole around its neck and led it away.

When Arthur tried to seize the tunic that the Patriarch of Jerusalem gave to St. Padern, the earth swallowed him up to his chin and held him until he begged forgiveness.

Glastonbury's first connection with Arthur appears in the *Life of Gildas* written in Geoffrey of Monmouth's time. Early sections describe Arthur's killing of Gildas' brother Hoel during military activities in Scotland, but the saint forgave the soldier later on when Gildas was in Somerset at Glastonbury Abbey. Melvas, ruler of the region, abducted Guenevere to his marsh-surrounded stronghold at Glastonbury. As Arthur and his men moved to besiege it, the Abbot and Gildas intervened to prevent bloodshed. Melvas restored Guenevere, and both kings gave lands to the Abbey.

From then on, successive abbots were increasingly appreciative of Arthur.

The area called the Isle of Avalon possesses—is possessed by—a mystique that attracted human veneration long before the beginning of recorded time in Britain. It is no figurative island. Until recent centuries, the territory between the Mendip and the Quantock Hills, extending far inland from Bristol Channel, was a marsh across which only those who knew secret hidden causeways could travel. The Romans who engineered the Fosse Way carried it across Somerset's marshes on a high embankment. As late as the 19th century the sea broke in on more than one occasion and spread a brackish flood over miles of flat pasture now squared by rows of willows growing on the dykes of multitudinous canals.

Yet even when most of the area lay chronically under shallow water, it was not only occupied but used as a center for wide-spread trade. At Meare, not far from the Glastonbury abbots' later fish house, and near Godney, still closer to Glastonbury, numerous adjacent small humps were observed and excavated last century; they proved to mark lake villages of the La Tène culture, occupied from the 3rd century B.C. until a mid-1st century raid by the Belgae all but annihilated their population.

Built on platforms topping piles driven vertically into the marsh, and reached by causeways, these settlements developed a diversified

economy. In addition to hunting and fishing, they grew cereals and raised sheep and cattle; their manufactures ranged from wheeled carts to glass beads with inlaid patterns. A seventeen-foot boat hollowed from an oak, now in the Glastonbury museum, exhibits their means of transport; their cargoes and the distances travelled in the course of their trade are witnessed by artifacts of tin, copper, iron, lead, glass and Kimmeridge shale. Their jewelry and bowls of metal and clay are fine examples of design; bone dice hint how they spent leisure hours.

Out of the marsh where these settlements were located, Tor Hill rises in a sudden cone, a pervasive presence above the flat landscape. It can be seen from the southeast, from the ramparts of the hill fort at South Cadbury called Camelot. It can be seen from the southwest, where a similar hill called Burrow Mump, topped by castle ruins, protects a milder rise on which King Alfred is reputed to have neglected the cakes and recorded to have assembled his army against the Danes in 818.

To the northwest, the Tor fronts the Mendip Hills where native islanders around Priddy mined lead for Mediterranean buyers centuries before Christ. The Roman operations initiated at Charterhouse six years after the invasion exploited diggings already old.

To the Celts, the Tor symbolized the myth of the agricultural year: they held it to be the castle of Gwyn son of Nudd, god of the underworld; every May Day morning he fights with Gwythyr son of Greidyawl for the hand of Creuddylad (Cordelia), daughter of the sun god Llud.

Excavations on the Tor in 1964–66 unearthed evidence of long human presence. The small finds ranged from Mesolithic and Neo-

171

lithic flints and a stone ax-head through Roman pottery and post-Roman ceramics from the Mediterranean, mostly wine and olive jars, to a 6th century bronze head.

Traces of timber buildings appeared from many periods, including 6th century postholes and timber slots. While these may indicate a monastic site, the many food bones found beside them suggest meat-eating secular occupants, who could have manned a military outpost contemporary with defenses at South Cadbury.

Identification of early Celtic monasteries is difficult: in Ireland, Wales, and at sites such as Tintagel and Glastonbury, the cells of the first monks consisted of small, separate wattled huts, or occasionally caves, very like those depicted in illumined manuscripts; these, a church, an abbot's cell and a hospice were enclosed within a rough wall. The Welsh name for the whole was 'Llan'-enclosure; place names like Llangollen—the Llan of Colin, or Llancarvan—the Llan of Garvan, combine the word for enclosure with the name of the saint who founded it. Because of their light construction and small size, the existence of such establishments is hard to confirm archaeologically until the sturdier monastic structures familiar from later years make their appearance.

On the Tor, monastic use becomes definite in the 10th–12th centuries. The present tower that accentuates the height of this landmark is what a 13th century earthquake left of a chapel to St. Michael.

The derivation of Glastonbury's name evokes old mysteries. The area was early referred to as Ynis Witrin, the island of glass. Since the Celtic Otherworld was frequently conceived as a Glass Tower, when the name spread to France Chrétien de Troyes made Melwas (Meleagant) the king of the Otherworld. Translation of Ynis Witrin into Glastonbury, however, runs afoul of the Anglo-Saxon possibility that this was Glaesting burgh, the town of the Glaesting family.

A visual explanation is given by an anonymous 18th century antiquary:

> The old Britons called this place Yniswitrin, which afterwards the Saxons interpreted into Glastonbury, or the Town of Glass; so called on account of the river's encompassing of the marsh, as clear as crystal,

and as it were, of the colour of glass. It was likewise called Avalonia, or the Isle of Avalon: it had the name of an island on account of being formerly enclosed about by a deep marsh; and Avalon, either from the British word Avale, signifying Apples, because it abounded with apple-trees when it was cleared from woods and bushes, and first made habitable, or else from one Avalon, who was once Lord of that territory.

Even today, the canals that have replaced the marshes mirror as in a glass magnificent reflections of cloud and sky.

Christian legends about early occupants of the Tor and the abbey grounds range westward to Ireland, eastward to the Mediterranean, and backward in time to the first century of the Christian era; even in more recent days they have been augmented from century to century.

In addition to the Irish hermits believed to have long occupied the Tor, St. Patrick was held to have returned from Ireland either to establish or to enter an already existing monastery on the flat land below, and to have died there in 472. Fifth century occupancy of the Abbey land, and the relation of such occupants to those at South Cadbury, is, however, conjectural. The first historically firm date for a foundation is that of King Ina after the West Saxons were in control.

But for centuries before his day, a wattled church some sixty by twenty feet in size stood where St. Mary's Chapel stands now, described as "an oratory of bark and Alder or wicker wands, winded and twisted together, with a Roof of Straw, or rather, after the nature of the Soil of the Neighbourhood, of Hay or Rushes."

One legend made Jesus himself the builder of this 'vetusta ecclesia'; others, derived from the French chronicles, dated it from the 1st century coming of Joseph of Arimathea.

This deeply venerated edifice, together with practically all of the surrounding monastery, was destroyed by fire in 1184.

Prompt rebuilding was essential. Henry II patronized the replacement, sending one of his chamberlains to speed the work. The Chapel of St. Mary, with dimensions the same as the wattled church and put on its site, was dedicated in 1189—its walls, carved Romanesque portals and interlaced arches stand today. But Henry II died in 1189, and

Richard Coeur de Lion had heart—and funds—only for his Crusade. The need for a new financial source was pressing.

Yet by 1193, further work was well in hand: the monks had tapped a fresh supply of revenue. In their cemetery, they had discovered the graves of Arthur and Guenevere.

This was the French romancers' high moment of popularity and circulation. The noble public for whom they wrote moved throughout the Plantagenet domain. Wealthy pilgrimages to relics of the rulers of the greatest court of chivalry were assured. Within months of the exhumation, King Richard himself, in Sicily, presented a sword said to be Excalibur to Tancred, the Norman ruler there.

174

A close-to-first-hand account of the discovery was written by Gerald of Wales, a chronicler who visited Glastonbury in 1192–3 and was shown Arthur's tomb. He was told that Henry II himself, relying on the advice of a Welsh bard, had urged the abbot to dig between 'two pyramids' in the monks' cemetery. (The 'pyramids' were reported in existence as late as the end of the 18th century; they seem to have been tapered plinths inscribed with a roster of early saints and abbots.)

Now the body of King Arthur, which legend had feigned to have been transferred at his passing, as it were in ghostly form, by spirits to a distant place and to have been exempt from death, was found in these our days at Glastonbury deep down in earth and encoffined in a hollow oak between two stone pyramids erected long ago in the consecrated graveyard, the site being revealed by strange and almost miraculous signs; and it was afterwards transported with honour to the Church and decently consigned to a marble tomb. Now in the grave there was found a cross of lead, placed under a stone and not

175

above it, as is now customary, but fixed to the lower side. This cross I myself have seen; for I have felt the letters engraved thereon, which do not project or stand out, but are turned inwards toward the stone. They run as follows:

HERE LIES BURIED THE RENOWNED KING ARTHUR
WITH GUENEVERE HIS SECOND WIFE
IN THE ISLAND OF AVALON

Now in regard to this there are many things worthy of note. For he had two wives, the last of whom was buried with him, and her bones were found together with his, but separated from them as thus; two parts of the tomb, to wit, the head, were alloted to the bones of the man, while the remaining third towards the foot contained the bones of the woman in a place apart; and there was found a tress of woman's hair still retaining its colour and its freshness; but when a certain monk snatched it and lifted it with greedy hand, it straightway all of it fell into dust. Now whereas there were certain indications in their writings that the body would be found there, and others in the letters engraven upon the pyramids, though they were much defaced by their extreme age, and others again were given in visions and revelations vouchsafed to good men and religious, yet it was above all King Henry II of England that most clearly informed the monks, as he had heard from an ancient Welsh bard, a singer of the past, that they would find the body at least sixteen feet beneath the earth, not in a tomb of stone, but in a hollow oak. And this is the reason why the body was placed so deep and hidden away, to wit, that it might not by any means be discovered by the Saxons who occupied the island after his death, whom he had so often in his life defeated and almost utterly destroyed; and for the same reason those letters, witnessing to the truth, that were stamped upon the cross, were turned inwards towards the stone, that they might at that time conceal what the tomb contained, and yet in due time and place might some day reveal the truth.

Like the 'pyramids', the leaden cross survived into the 18th century; in 1607 the antiquary Camden published a drawing of both the cross and its inscriptions: he gives the latter as HIC JACET SEPULTUS INCLITUS REX ARTHURIUS IN INSULA AVALONIA. The hollowed oak coffin raises a query: could the monks, in digging, have happened across a boat from the lake villages?

The Tudor antiquary Bale communicates the excitement of the exhumation even more vividly than Gerald:

> In Avallon, in 1191, there found they the flesh bothe of Arthur and of hys wyfe Guenever turned all into duste, wythin theyr coffines of strong oke, the bones only remaynynge. A monke of the same abbeye, standyng and behouldyng the fine broydinges of the womman's hear as *yellow as golde* there still to remayne, as a man ravyshed, or more than halfe from his wyttes, he leaped into the graffe, xv fote depe, to have caugte them sodenlye. But he fayled of his purpose. For so soon as they were touched they fell all to powder.

The bodies were reinterred in the new church. Almost a century later, in a colorful ceremony at Eastertide of 1278, painted chests with the alleged remains were opened in the presence of King Edward I and placed in an imposing monument before the high altar at a spot still marked in the Abbey ruins.

This tomb disappeared in the wreckage of the Dissolution, but two descriptions of it remain. One is a verse from the book of Ruben of Bath:

> *At Glastonbury on the queer*
> *They made Artourez toumbe there,*
> *And wrote with latyn vers thus*
> HIC JACET ARTHURUS, REX QUONDAM REXQUE FUTURUS.

The antiquary Leland cites a different epitaph. Between Edmund the Elder and Edmund Ironside, he says,

> lay Arthur with this simple epitaph:
>
> HIC JACET ARTURUS, FLOS REGUM, GLORIA REGNI,
> QUEM MORES, PROBITAS COMMENDANT LAUDI PERENNI.

177

He notes that the head of the monument was carved with a figure of the abbot under whom the discovery was made, holding a crucifix; at the foot, a figure of Arthur. There was

> a cross on the tomb; and two lions at the head, and two at the feet, reaching to the ground. At his feet, his Queen, with this epitaph:
>
> ARTURI JACET HIC CONJUX TUMULATA SECUNDA,
> QUAE MERUIT CAELOS VIRTUTEM PROLE FECUNDA.

The references to Guenevere as Arthur's second wife are puzzling, but they have a companion in Welsh literature; the *Record of a Conversation between King Arthur and his Second Wife Guenevere* is a coy bit of persiflage in which she remarks, "I saw a well-built man at Arthur's long table in Dyfnaint sharing out wine to friends," and he replies, "That's where you saw me!"

In the course of the 13th century, history began to be corrected to provide background for the Arthurian finds. Before long, William of Malmesbury began to be quoted in substantiation of the burial; some sixty years before the exhumation he had written a book *On the Antiquity of the Church of Glastonbury*, and relevant passages were now found to be part of it. But recent scholarship has identified them as insertions, in the script of a number of medieval hands. Suspicion as to one of the authors points in the direction of Adam of Domersham: all of the material added to William's text appears in his late 13th century *History of Events at Glastonbury*, and he may have had access to the Cambridge manuscript in which the newly-identified insertions appear. The pseudo-William is made to state:

> I forebear to speak of Arthur, the famous king of the Britons, who is buried with his queen in the cemetery of the monks, between two pyramids. . . . In the year 542 this Arthur was mortally wounded by Modred in Cornwall near the river Camba, and carried to the isle of Avalon to be healed of his wounds; and there he died in the summer-time, at about whitsuntide, being about a hundred years old.

178

A gloss in a different script affirms:

After the battle of Kemelen in Cornwall, at which Arthur was mortally wounded and Modred was killed (Modred was that wicked traitor who usurped the throne of Britain entrusted to his care, against Arthur his uncle), the wounded Arthur was carried to the Isle of Avalon (now called Glaston) by a certain noble dame, his kinswoman, called Morganis. And when he died he was buried, by her good offices, in the cemetery of the monks.

This is the origin of the fable commonly told by the fable-telling Britons and their bards, that an absurd fairy called Morganis brought the wounded Arthur to the Isle of Avalon to be healed of his wounds. And when his wounds are healed the king will come back in his majesty and might to rule over the Britons as formerly (they say). And so they wait his coming to this day, as the Jews await the coming of their Messiah; and they surpass the Jews themselves in their fatuity and infidelity and in their vain imaginings.

And a third insertion names Arthur as the benefactor of Glastonbury:

You may read among the deeds of the most glorious Arthur that one Christmas Day he had knighted at Caerleon a very stalwart young man called Ider, son of prince Nuth, and went out with him to the Mount of Frogs, now called Brent Knoll, to slay three giants who were notorious for their evil deeds there.

The young knight went on in front of Arthur and his companions, and lost touch with them; and courageously falling upon the giants, heroically slew them.

When the fight was over, Arthur came up and found the said Ider quite overcome by his too great toil, and lying exhausted and unconscious. So Arthur and his companions began to mourn for his death. And Arthur turned homewards sad at heart, leaving the body there till he could give instructions for a cart to bring it in. And feeling himself responsible for the young man's death, because he had delayed too long upon the road, when at last he reached Glastonbury he appointed twenty-four monks to pray for Ider's soul, and bestowed gifts on them in abundance: lands for their support, gold and silver, and altar-vessels and other church-ornaments.

179

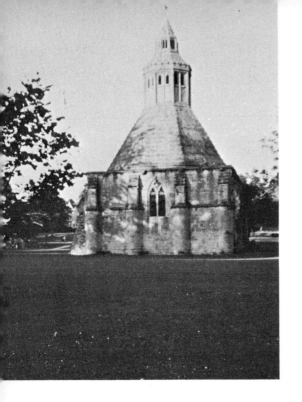

Glastonbury was long known as the place of one of Britain's
three perpetual choirs; a Welsh triad lists:

> One was at the Island of Afallach [Avalon],
> and the second at Caer Garadawg,
> and the third at Bangor.
>
> In each of these three places there were 2,400 religious men; and of
> these 100 in turn continued each hour of the twenty-four hours of the
> day and night in prayer and service to God, ceaselessly and without
> rest forever.)

A final notation in William's manuscript specifies the lands given
by Arthur and Melwas to the Abbey, saying that "these properties
were Brent (thus delivered from the Giants) and Shapwick and lands
adjoining." Brent Knoll is a hill similar to the Tor further west by
Bristol Channel; at Shapwick, much closer to Glastonbury, excavations were initiated in the summer of 1967 in the hope of finding
5th and 6th century artifacts.

By 1303 the main outlines of the great new church were sub-

stantially complete, though successive abbots made additions almost
to the time of the Dissolution. The final grandeur of its nearly six
hundred foot extent was as resplendent as that of any abbey in England;
ruins of its transeptual arches and remaining outlines still convey
a shadow of its majesty.

To the east of the church were cloisters, dorter, refectory; the
nearby kitchen, intact because used as a dwelling after the Dissolution, was supplied from the conveniently close Abbot's Barn, where
cattle ruminate in the barnyard now, and the Abbot's Fish House near
Meare; the monks were likewise endowed with numerous nearby
farms, and enjoyed such emoluments as their annual six-day fair on
the summit of the Tor—even now, a secular one-day fair is held on
September 19 at the Fairfield.

The town beside the Abbey still displays the tribunal where the
abbot dispensed justice, today a museum; one of the inns where pil-
grims stayed then and visitors stay now; and the parish churches of
St. John and St. Benedict.

Where the road comes into the town from the southwest, the

181

bridge over the Avon is known to have been called Pomparles as early as 1415. The name is a corruption of 'pont perilleux'; Leland called it "Pontperlus, wher men fable that Arture cast in his sword." But other places also vaunt themselves as the site where an arm clothed in white samite caught Excalibur as it arced above the water—among them are Dozmary Pool on Bodmin Moor in Cornwall and Llyn Llydaw on the Snowdon massif in Wales.

This is how it came to pass that two rival accounts described the end of the Arthurian epic: the Glastonbury monks' version of a burial and various romancers' version of a mysterious passage to the same Isle of Avalon not followed by death.

A chronicle written around 1205 by Layamon, an English priest at Arley Regis on the Severn in Worcestershire, tells of the passing: Arthur, desperately wounded at Camelford, after committing his realm to Cador of Cornwall, says:

And I will fare to Avalun, to the fairest of all maidens, to Argante the queen, an elf most fair, and she shall make my wounds all sound; make me all whole with healing draughts. And afterwards I will come again to my kingdom, and dwell with the Britons with mickle joy.

The 14th century English *Le Morte Arthure* corroborates the monks in telling of a burial. At a manor in Avalon

A surgeon from Salerno   searches his wounds;
The king sees by testing   that he will never be sound,
And at once to his faithful men   he utters these words:

183

'Call me a confessor,   *with Christ in his arms;*
I shall be houseled in haste,   *whatso may betide me . . . . . .*
   He said 'In manus tuas'   *on the earth where he lies,*
And thus passes his spirit,   *and he speaks no more.*
The baronage of Britain then,   *bishops and others,*
Go to Glastonbury   *with grieving hearts,*
To bury their bold king,   *and bring him to earth,*
With all honor and richness   *that any man should have.*
Sadly toll the bells,   *and sing requiem,*
Say masses and matins,   *with mournful notes;*
The religious vest them   *in their rich copes,*
Pontiffs and prelates   *in precious vestments;*
Dukes and douzepers   *in their coats of mourning;*
Countesses kneeling,   *and clasping their hands,*
Ladies languishing,   *and sorrowful in appearance.*

But if the discovery of Arthur and Guenevere's tomb was an immediate financial asset to the Abbey at the time of the fire, the legend of Joseph of Arimathea was of practical value in prestige and precedence over several centuries.

The tradition transmitted by Freculfe's 9th century chronicle set the date of arrival of the mission headed by Joseph and dispatched by the apostle Philip as the year 65.

A slightly different popular belief, stubbornly held in Somerset, insists that Joseph came directly to England from the Near East as a merchant engaged in the metal trade, and that during the unrecorded years of Jesus' young manhood, He came with him. Not only does archaeology substantiate such a commerce as existing from prehistoric times; the lead miners of the Mendip Hills, whose diggings were worked from antiquity until very recently, had a saying, "As sure as Christ came to Priddy." Their warning cry when about to pour molten metal was, "Just as Joseph did!"

As to the relics that Joseph brought with him, one version has him carry the chalice in which the wine was drunk at the Last Supper and which became the Holy Grail, but another endows him with two cruets containing the blood and sweat of the crucified Christ.

According to Welsh lore in Cardiganshire, what Joseph brought was definitely the chalice. The Nanteos family near Aberystwyth possesses a bowl of olivewood; the Glastonbury monks are said to have smuggled it over the mountains at the time of the Dissolution into the keeping of the abbey of Strata Florida. When these monks were ejected, in turn, the Powell family sheltered them. Their last

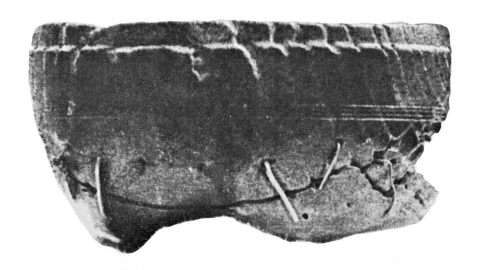

survivor gave the cup to the head of the house, saying that in sickness, a drink from it would cure. Down subsequent centuries, many sufferers have asked to be sent water poured from the Nanteos bowl.

Closer to Glastonbury, earlier preference was for the cruets, though in recent years a Chalice Well on the lower slopes of the Tor has invited visitors to the spring that used to supply the Abbey's water. Richard Bere, the last abbot to complete his tenure undisturbed, adopted the cruets as part of a new abbatical device. (Abbot Whiting, who followed him, was hanged, drawn and quartered on Tor Hill when the minions of Henry VIII seized the property in 1539.)

The Bere blazon has a white field diapered with red drops representing the holy blood; the cruets appear below the arms of a green cross formed by two staves from which branches have been lopped off on either side. The device appears in stone on the outside wall of the former almshouse chapel west of the Abbey and on a battlement of

the Church of St. Benedict, in wood on the boss of a beam in the same church, and in stained glass in the south window of the chancel of St. John's. It was Abbot Bere who built the Chapel of St. Joseph in the crypt of the Lady Chapel, recently restored to oecumenic use.

Joseph himself carries the cruets in the late 15th century glass of the east window of the parish church at Langport, southwest of Glastonbury. The church is on a rise overlooking the ruins of Muchelney Abbey; a carving there shows the parish priest holding tight to the allotment of bread and wine that his appointment specified he should receive daily from the Abbey kitchen.

Joseph with his cruets is depicted a second time on a painted panel in the Perpendicular rood screen of the exquisite parish church in the village of Plymtree near Cullompton in Devon.

Glastonbury's more recent creators of legend have also been inspired by the staff Joseph carried on arrival. A 16th century rhyme on the wonders of the place contains the first reference to the Christmas-

187

blooming thorn, though a 14th century seal of the Abbey shows the Virgin holding a hawthorn bush:

> *Three Hawthorns also, that groweth in Werrall*
> *Do burge and bear green leaves at Christmas*
> *As fresh as other in May. . . .*

The tree, *crataegus oxyacantha praecox,* does indeed bloom early in January, the time of Christmas before calendar reform. At present there is a thriving example in the Abbey grounds, while a wind-blown replant struggles on the hill above Pomparles bridge. The hill was named Wearyall as the legend grew that the thorn sprouted from a staff that Joseph stuck into the ground at the end of his long journey.

    The tree on the hill has had a rugged history. In Elizabeth's reign, a Puritan took an ax to it, but the ax is said to have rebounded to cut his leg while a chip injured his eye. The tree resumed growth, only to be chopped down by Cromwellians in the Civil War; the antiquary Robert Plot explains their reason: "some take it for a miraculous re-membrance of the birth of Christ, first planted by Joseph of Arima-thea." Eighteenth century replants were successively destroyed by souvenir hunters, to the indignation of a local resident, John Clark, who placed a stone, still located near the present tree, carved with the legend: *J. A. Anno D. XXXI.*

If 'J. A.' brought the chalice or the cruets with him, his coming could hardly have been as early as the year 31, but his arrival in the second half of the 1st century was solidly and successfully defended by the Glastonbury abbots as the basis of their precedence, both in the protocol of the English church (in which St. Albans eventually displaced them) and in a quarrel which occupied four successive oecumenic councils, at Pisa in 1409, at Constance in 1417, at Siena in 1424, and at Basel ten years later.

A late 18th century antiquary's *History and Antiquities of Glastonbury, collected from various authors, and to which is added, an account of* THE MINIRAL WATERS, *and of the Glastonbury Thorn,* published when visits to such spas as Bath were at the height of upper-class popularity, lists cures, attested by affidavits, attributed to the waters of St. Joseph's well in the crypt of the Lady Chapel. Certified recoveries name human ills from asthma and running ulcers to the king's evil and leprosy. The tract includes the advice:

> *Ye sick, to Glaston come away,*
> *Here is no Doctor's bill to pay;*
> *This healing water will procure*
> *An eleomosynary cure.*

Very shortly after Glastonbury's original Arthurian discoveries, Continental writers began to hear of them. The author of the *Perlesvaus,* whose dialect places him in North France or Belgium, says he translates into French a Latin book from the "holy house in the Isle of Avalon at the head of the Adventurous Marshes." He might have been supplied at Fécamp on the Channel coast north of Le Havre —the Benedictines of Glastonbury had a sister establishment there.

This author certainly seems familiar with a number of West Country and Welsh sites: he refers to Dinas Bran and has either visited or heard vividly described the castle at Tintagel:

189

Therewithal Perceval departeth from the Damsel, without saying more, and rideth until he cometh to the kingdom of Wales to a castle that is seated above the sea upon a high rock, and it is called the Castle of Tallages. . . . He entereth into the first baily of the castle, and alighteth at the mounting-stage, and setteth down his shield and his spear, and looketh toward the steps whereby one goes up to the higher hall.

On another occasion in the same tale, Lancelot sees the tombs at Glastonbury: he

left his arms without the chapel and entereth therein, and saith that never has he seen none so fair nor so rich. There were within three other places, right fair and seemly dight of rich cloths of silk and rich corners and fringes of gold. He seeth the images and the crucifixes all newly fashioned, and the chapel illumined of rich colours; and moreover in the midst thereof were two coffins, one against the other and at the four corners four tall wax tapers burned that were right rich, in four right rich candlesticks. The coffins were covered with two palls, and there were clerks that chanted psalms in turn on the one side and the other. 'Sir', saith Lancelot to one of the hermits, 'For whom were these coffins made?' 'For King Arthur and Queen Guinievre?' 'King Arthur is not yet dead,' saith Lancelot. 'No, in truth, please God! but the body of the Queen lieth in the coffin before us, and in the other is the head of her son, until such time as the King shall be ended, to whom God grant long life!'

But if the *Perlesvaus* text found its origin in Glastonbury, Glastonbury was quick to contest one of its incidents. The author says that Ywain's son, while still a squire, found and brought to Arthur a magnificent gold candlestick: "King Arthur, with the approval of Ywain his father, gave the candlestick to S. Paul in London, for the church was newly founded. . . . ." But at the Abbey, the monk John of Glastonbury told the tale another way: the candlestick remained in the locality and was deposited with the Irish brethren at the nearby hermitage of Beckery.

VIII

REPATRIATION
OF THE
LEGENDS

For two centuries after the Norman Conquest, the Anglo-Norman overlay of French- and Latin-speaking king and nobles, bishops and upper clergy required no other language for their literature. Indeed, most of them had small occasion to become fluent in anything else.

Yet some of the French romances had British authors—the *Lancelot, Quest of the Grail,* and *Mort Artu* of the prose 'Vulgate' cycle are credited to the partly Welsh Anglo-Norman courtier Walter Map, the witty court companion of Henry II whom miniaturists often show taking dictation from the king.

192   And as time went on the stubborn persistence in the British island of the speech familiar from the Anglo-Saxon conquest eventu-

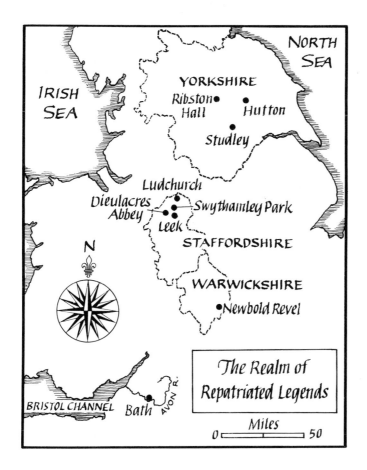

The Realm of Repatriated Legends

ally displaced the Normans' French—by Chaucer's day, throughout the island, the mother-tongue of literature as well as daily life was English.

As late as Edward III, a chronicler declared that "uplandish men will liken themselves to gentlemen and strive with great business for to speak French, for to be i-told of," but those who cared less about being 'i-told of' wanted something they could read in the dialect of their everyday speech. Consequently, since the romances remained popular, English authors engaged in increasingly massive translations from the French.

Most of the Arthurian stories told in the vernacular originated on the fringes of the Anglo-Norman world, the West Country, the

193

Midlands, Yorkshire, Scotland. Some authors revived the alliterative verse-forms imported at the time of *Beowulf*; others contented themselves with prose.

In general, they did not add new characters or episodes. The freshness of their versions comes in part from the occasional insights with which they turn stock characters into individuals, and in part from their closely observed descriptions of the countryside that give Arthur a realm of England.

For instance, the 14th century author who repatriated Percival under his old Welsh name of Peredur presents a recognizable adolescent instead of a conventional youth. Peredur's mother, having lost husband and elder sons through knightly combats, retires into the forest and there shelters her youngest from all knowledge of chivalry. But after some knights come riding by, the youth goes out into the world, bursting with curiosity while citing sayings of his mother. The kindly knight who instructs him in the use of arms and the conventions of chivalry counsels him to quote her less and ask fewer questions. Consequently, when he visits the castle of the Maimed King and sees the Grail procession pass, though yearning to know what it is all about, he refrains from asking his host the question that would have cured him.

A description of the unlikely situation when Arthur, who under cover of night has impersonated his sister's husband and begotten Modred upon her, tells her about it while waiting on her at high table ends with an observation that reveals the penetrating eye of a watchful and experienced courtier:

But the next day he told her himself at dinner when he served her at the table, kneeling.

'Sir squire, rise up,' she said, 'for you have been kneeling long enough.'

He answered softly, saying that he might never deserve the favors she had done him. She asked him what bounty it was that she had given him. He replied that he could never tell her unless she assured him she would in no way reveal it to any person, nor bring about harm or blame to him. She said that it would not grieve her, and promised him that she would not mind this thing. Then he told her how he had lain by her that night. The lady felt great shame and blushed deeply, but no one knew the cause. She lost her appetite completely.

The French writers usually describe a battle in terse, fast-moving narrative; some of the English chroniclers use scenic similes. In the *Brut* of Maistre Wace of Caen, the Roman tribune, Frollo, dies at Paris in single combat with Arthur. After being felled by a two-handed blow from Excalibur, flat on the ground, he "beating the earth a little with his chausses of steel, presently died, and was still."

By contrast, in the *Brut* of the English monk Layamon, as the battle of Badon is joined at Bath where the River Avon flows around the hill, reflections of the opposing armies appear in the stream:

Then yet called Arthur, noblest of kings: 'Yesterday was Baldulf of all knights boldest, but now he standeth on the hill, and beholdeth the Avon, how the steel fishes lie in the stream! Armed with sword, their life is destroyed; their scales float like gold-dyed shields; there float their fins, as if it were spears. These are marvelous things come to this land; such beasts on the hill, such fishes in the stream!'

Occasionally, even when an author does not specify the spot which he describes, his words correspond so closely to an identifiable setting as to induce certainty that this is the place he had in mind. The geography of the late 14th century poet who wrote *Sir Gawain and the Green Knight* in alliterative verse and a south Midlands dialect invites exploration of the countryside just above Leek in Staffordshire.

At Arthur's Christmas court in Camelot, a Green Knight on a green horse issues a challenge to a beheading test, he to receive a blow of a battle-ax forthwith and unresisting, but to be entitled to return it in a year and a day. Gawain accepts the challenge; his stroke severs the Green Knight's head. Picking up his head, the Knight remounts, tells Gawain to be sure to meet him at the Green Chapel, and rides away. On the appointed day, Gawain keeps his rendezvous.

Events at Dieulacres Abbey, some eight miles north of Leek, in the year 1380 may have given the author of *Sir Gawain* his opening theme. The earls of Chester had a hunting lodge at Swythamley Park; one night Earl Ranulf III had a dream in which his grandfather instructed him to establish a Cistercian house nearby—he anticipated the design of the west front of Bath Abbey by specifying that "there is to be built a stairway by which descending and ascending angels may offer the prayers of men and convey grace."

Turning to his wife Clementia, Ranulf told her of his dream: in her Norman French she exclaimed, "Deux encres! (May God prosper it!)", and the Abbey received its name.

The establishment that took form over the years, constructed from the pink local stone, was commodious and well endowed. But wealth from the wool trade made the monks worldly: quarreling over boundaries multiplied; celebration of offices grew lax.

In 1380, the abbot's retainers committed a heinous crime. The previous year, a royal order had initiated an investigation into the allegation that the abbot and his men had committed assaults and even murders. The abbot accused a local citizen of "assaulting his servants, wounding them so badly that their services were lost to him for a time." His retainers laid in wait for this man and wounded him; after the fracas he was taken to Leek gaol. Then, after consultation with their superior, the retainers raided the gaol and took him up onto Leek Moor. There, they beheaded him.

The moor presents some of the wildest scenery in England. Black crags known as edges, 'gnarled rough knuckles of rock', cleave cloud or sky. Their very name, The Roaches, catches a translator's ear: it is an anglicization of 'rochères'. In seconds, vast storms sweep across them from the west, obliterating their every outline.

Gawain, seeking the Green Chapel, looked on such a landscape:

Now the New Year draws near, and the night passes,
The day dispels the dark, by the Lord's decree;

But wild weather awoke in the world without:
The clouds in the cold sky cast down their snow
With great gusts from the north, grievous to bear.
Sleet showered aslant upon shivering beasts;
The wind warbled wild as it whipped from aloft,
And drove the drifts deep in the dales below.

Below the moor, in a deep ravine, the Black Brook and the Dane
River converge at Forest Bottom. There, ruinous walls top a mound
that old maps show to have been a forge built by the monks of Dieulacres Abbey; the present footbridge runs beside remains of a stone
structure still marked as Castor's Bridge. Here the poet could have
heard the fine whetting sound that Gawain hears as the Green Knight,
preparing for the rendezvous, puts an edge on his Danish ax.

A site for the Green Chapel where the two meet is in the ravine
above the forge. In the 17th century, Robert Plot said that the
place had long been known as Lud's Church or Ludchurch; local
legend reputed it to have served as a hiding place for Lollards, a haunt
of headless riders, the lair of a tall man in Lincoln green.

Without warning, a delta-shaped cleft beside a trail gives entrance to a rock chamber whose black walls, open to the sky, rise vertically to a height of twenty feet. A step-like passage descends to a deeper level where spring water quickens a crack in the narrow floor, so cold that the air above it condenses into rising swirls of mist when struck by a shaft of sun. In microscopic cracks, close-growing grasses, ferns and moss splash the black rock with incandescent green.

Compare the account of Gawain's entry:

199

It had a hole at one end, and on either side,
And was covered with coarse grass in clumps all without,
And hollow all within, like some old cave,
Or a crevice of an old crag—he could not discern
                    aright.

  "Can this be the Chapel Green?
  Alack!" said the man, "Here might
  The devil himself be seen
  Saying matins at black midnight!"

Such descriptions localized various Arthurian stories once more in their country of origin. The greatest single event in the repatriation of the legends, however, was the compilation of the entire cycle in the second half of the 15th century in English under the name of *Le Morte Darthur.*

Oddly enough, the elusiveness of firm fact that plagues the historic Arthur from Gildas' first oblique references persists even to this final and comprehensive translation. The work is known to have been written in the latter 1460's by a man whose name was Sir Thomas Malory—that much is vouchsafed by the colophon of the first edition, published by William Caxton in 1485. But who was Thomas Malory?

Within the past eighty years the search for details about the man, his life and his sources has unearthed much new material. Previously, information was limited to a reference in *Chief Illustrious Writers of Britain,* published by John Bale in 1548, which quotes Leland as an authority for Malory being of Welsh descent.

But his identity has not been settled. In the 1890's George Lyman Kittredge found a Sir Thomas Malory who lived at Newbold Revel in Warwickshire; he became his persuasive advocate. Until the present decade, it is to this man that authorship has generally been ascribed.

Generally, but gingerly. As researchers document more and more facts about his life, his candidacy appears more and more unsuitable.

His positive qualifications are that he was a knight of the right time; that he was alive in 1469-70, the year—the ninth of Edward IV's

reign—in which at the close of his work the author says that he finished his book; and that he died, as Caxton says the author has done,
before the work was printed in 1485.

The drawbacks of his biography are several. During the 1440's
and 1450's he was convicted of an extraordinary range of crimes, from
cattle stealing to rape to attempted murder, and served considerable
time in various gaols, first in the provinces, where he broke out with
repeated facility, and later in the Marshalsea at Southwark and Lydgate
and Newgate in London.

From one point of view, his imprisonments seem to substantiate
his statement at the end of an early section of his book that it was
"drawyn by a knyght presoner", and his requests to his readers,
scattered through the text, to pray that "God sende hym good delyv-
eraunce sone and hastely." But as more work has been done on the
dates when he was in gaol, his needs for deliverance do not seem to
coincide with the period when he was writing—during the latter
1460's, he was apparently at large.

Furthermore, while he was alive at the date at which he says he
completed the book—though he lived for only one more year—he
would have been, especially for medieval times, a quite elderly author.
He is known to have served as a mercenary at Calais attached to
Richard Beauchamp, Earl of Warwick, who was named Captain of
Calais in 1414–15 and who died in 1439. He represented his county
in Parliament; he was knighted in 1445.

His association with successive earls of Warwick, moreover, raises
a question regarding his politics. The text of the *Morte Darthur* is
Lancastrian in tone; Warwick the kingmaker, though a man of supple
allegiance, was chief manipulator of the Yorkist cause. If Malory the
author was Warwick's man, why should he have been specifically
excluded from a general pardon granted by the Yorkist king, Edward
IV, in 1468?

Some critics point to this knight's turbulent life as assorting ill
with the moral indignation expressed at times in the *Morte Darthur*.
In prison or out, a man with his record might be expected thought-

fully to chew the end of his quill after putting into Lancelot's mouth such a speech as: "What? . . . is he a theff and a knyght? and a ravyssher of women? He doth shame unto the Order of Knyghthode, and contrary to his oath. Hit is pyté that he lyvyth." Yet this point should perhaps not be overly labored: Lancelot was introduced to German literature when Hugo de Morville brought a romance to Vienna when he came as a hostage replacing Richard Coeur de Lion in prison,—de Morville was one of Thomas à Becket's murderers.

Uncertainty as to facts about Malory has until very recently been paralleled by a complete absence of his manuscript text: for close to 450 years after Caxton's typesetter had the *Morte Darthur* in his composing room, no trace had been found.

Then in 1934, W. F. Oakeshott located a manuscript at Winchester College. Studied and published by Eugène Vinaver, it permits a view of the book free of Caxton's editorial cuts and divisions of material. This text, more complete at several points than the printed version, appears not to be the one that Caxton used.

During the same years, other scholars were canvassing records of other Malory families, trying to find another Thomas of appropriate date. In 1966, a new candidate for the authorship was brought forward by William Matthews, who drew the title for his *Ill-framed Knight* from Vinaver's observation about the Malory name: "it is not unlikely that the name has its origin in the Old French verb *orer* (= to frame, to surround) and that *Maloret* was a nickname meaning 'ill-framed' or 'ill-set'."

The new Thomas Malory is one of the younger sons of William and Dionisia Malory of Hutton and Studley near Ripon in Yorkshire. His life, like his namesake's in Warwickshire, offers both positive qualifications and drawbacks. His name is right; yet he is a younger son not specifically named as a knight in various pertinent documents. His age is more likely: he would have been in his mid-thirties when he completed his book. Since his neighborhood was Lancastrian in temper, it is not surprising to see his name in the list of exceptions to Edward IV's pardon—but the reference in the pardons is to a knight.

And though the author of the *Morte Darthur* repeatedly refers to himself as a prisoner, no court record of this Malory has been found.

One of Matthews' main reliances in advancing this man as the probable author is textual. At the time Malory wrote, English was becoming standardized, but regional dialects persisted, and Matthew's analysis of Malory's text shows him both familiar with and employing the speech characteristic of the North of England. While most of Malory's sources were French, he also drew on two English romances, the alliterative *Mort Arthure* and the stanzaic *Le Morte Arthur;* Matthews suggests that these texts would have offered no obstacles to a Yorkshireman but might have proved difficult for one from Warwickshire whose language was the English of central England. Other scholars counter with the point that Warwickshire seems more central today, divided from the north of England by the industrial Midlands, than it would have been before the industrial revolution.

Consideration also needs to be given to a manuscript found in a trunk at Ribston Hall, Wetherby, Yorkshire, and bought by Cambridge University Library in 1945. It was in a trunk with charters and other documents relative to the Mauleverer family, which owned this estate and intermarried with the same Yorkshire families as the Malorys of Hutton and Studley. The manuscript contains a *History of the Holy Grail* and a *Merlin*; the *Merlin* corresponds very closely to Malory's translation. An intriguing note at the top of one of its folios, in a late 15th or early 16th century hand, is keyed to a cross in the margin beside the description of Uther Pendragon's attraction to Igerna. The note reads: "Si coɱence le livre que Sir Thomas Malori Chr reduce in Engloys et fuist emprente par Willɱ Caxton." (Here begins the book which Sir Thomas Malory put into English and which William Caxton printed.)

The opening words of Book I, Chapter I, of the original Caxton edition are:

It befell in the days of Uther Pendragon, when he was king of all England, and so reigned, that there was a mighty duke in Cornwall

Here begynneth the fyrſte hym. And the duke was named the du⸗

that held war against him a long time. And the duke was named the duke of Tintagil. And so by means King Uther sent for this duke, charging him to bring his wife with him, for she was called a fair lady, and a passing wise, and her name was called Igraine. So when the duke and his wife were come unto the king, by the means of great lords they were accorded both: the king liked and loved this lady well, and he made them great cheer out of measure, and desired to have lain by her.

But one mystery is equally tantalizing in the case of both of the Thomas Malorys so far discovered: where did they obtain the French manuscripts necessary to so vast a translation? Matthews is doubtful whether any individual or institution in England had a collection rich enough to provide the required texts.

Adherents of Sir Thomas Malory of Newbold Revel suggest that when he was in Newgate the prison authorities may have facilitated his use of the library that Dick Whittington had recently established nearby in the Greyfriars monastery. But even if Malory's previous

204

record of successful escapes did not give his jailers pause, the likelihood of a religious establishment possessing a large collection of romances seems slim.

Matthews' comprehensive search has canvassed the contents of libraries on both sides of the Channel. Most tempting among the Arthurian collections in France is that belonging to the Jacques d'Armagnac who became duc de Nemours. In Paris, at the Biblio

205

thèque Nationale, and at other present-day libraries, nearly a hundred manuscripts once in his possession are known. Moreover, during the years 1460–70 his scribe Michel Gonnot compiled a giant manuscript of more than 1100 folios, of which the surviving three-quarters is now in the Bibliothèque Nationale, that gathered into one sequence the entire Arthurian cycle just as Malory did. Gonnot's work was finished in July 1470, only months after the completion of the *Morte Darthur*.

The certainties end too soon. The circumstances that caused Malory's exception from Edward IV's pardon might well have made residence abroad prudent; but if he spent part of the 1460's in France, and if a prisoner, why was he held, and where? The Malory mystery is a long way from being solved.

But no matter who wrote the *Morte Darthur,* its quality remains. The freshness of a May morning dews the day when Lancelot and Guenevere ride out from Joyous Gard. The dragon of Arthur's fore-boding dream before battle is as brilliant as the insignia of Wales. When Lancelot comes to the Amesbury nunnery, after the black barge of weeping ladies has borne the wounded Arthur away, Guene-vere's speech as the lovers bid each other farewell is the last pathetic word of the noble medieval chatelaines for whom the romances were created:

When Sir Launcelot was brought to her, then she said to all the ladies: Through this man and me hath all this war been wrought, and the death of the most noblest knights of the world; for through our love that we have loved together is my most noble lord slain. Therefore, Sir Launcelot, wit thou well that I am set in such a plight to get my soul heal; and yet I trust through God's grace that after my death to have a sight of the blessed face of Christ, and at domesday to sit on his right side, for as sinful as ever I was are saints in heaven. Therefore, Sir Launcelot, I require thee and

beseech thee heartily, for all the love that ever was betwixt us, that
thou never see me more in the visage; and I command thee, on God's
behalf, that thou forsake my company, and to thy kingdom thou turn
again, and keep well thy realm from war and wrake; for as well as I
have loved thee, mine heart will not serve me to see thee, for through
thee and me is the flower of kings and knights destroyed. . . . . .

The colophon of Caxton's first edition of the *Morte D'arthur*
reads:

Thus endeth this noble and joyous book entitled Le Morte Darthur.
Notwithstanding it treateth of the birth, life, and acts of the said King
Arthur, of his noble knights of the Round Table, their marvellous
enquests and adventures, the achieving of the Sangreal, and in the end
the dolorous death and departing out of the world of them all. Which
book was reduced into English by Sir Thomas Malory, knight, as
afore is said, and by me divided into twenty-one books, chaptered and
imprinted, and finished in the abbey Westminster the last day of July
the year of our Lord MCCCCLXXXV.

Caxton me fieri fecit.

Its success rivalled that of Geoffrey of Monmouth's chronicle nearly three hundred and fifty years earlier. A second edition was brought out in 1498, a third in 1529, a fourth in 1557; a centennial reprint appeared in 1585. Copies of all of these survive today.

The titles vary slightly: in several early editions they provide the fuller description of the contents that Caxton placed in the body of his colophon, as in *The Storye of the most noble and worthy Kynge Arthur imprinted by Thomas East, from Caxton.* Similarly, variations in some of the woodcuts—far cruder than the earlier handpainted miniatures—that serve as illustrations show Lancelot fighting a dragon that in one edition has one head and in another, three.

With this major retelling, the late medieval version of the Arthurian story took final form. Most of the 19th and 20th century revivals, in England and abroad, have Malory as their source.

AFTERWORD IX

DARK AGE
HEROES

My initial desire to explore the matter of Britain grew out of previous explorations of the matter of the ancient world. Less than a hundred years ago, the Trojan War of the 13th century B.C. was regarded as the literary creation of an imaginative bard or bards called Homer. But in the last half of the 19th century A.D. an amateur called Heinrich Schliemann dug and found Troy and dug again and unearthed Mycenae. In the first half of the 20th century knowledge of Mycenaean civilization was expanded by systematic excavation at both sites and by major discoveries at Pylos, Vaphio, Orchomenos, Thebes.

While history in Mycenaean times is still sparse, disbelief in the reality of its heroes has disappeared. The prehistoric Dark Age of the Eastern Mediterranean becomes brighter decade by decade.

In Britain, as in Asia Minor and Greece, fortuitous finds and planned digs have in recent years brought to light the new evidence on its Dark Age that I have summarized in this book. Only very lately

210

has the historic reality of Arthur been taken more than semi-seriously, yet John R. Morris of the University of London, one of the currently outstanding scholars of early British history and archaeology, is calling his new book *The Age of Arthur.*

Certain comparisons are striking. The historic times in which the Mycenaean and the Arthurian group of heroes lived are separated by some 1700 years. Yet both in their gay moments and in their grave hours, their stories are much the same.

The Arthurian heroes join with gusto in the boar hunt of Twrch Trwynt, chasing him across Wales, the Severn Estuary, and much of the West Country until he disappears in the sea off Cornwall. The Mycenaean heroes gather almost to a man to pursue the Calydonian boar, Aphareides, across northern Greece.

Audiences of both epics were entranced by meticulous descriptions of their heroes' armor, fashioned in both cases by superhuman craft, and of the great horses that ran before the war-chariots or charged into the lists. And they were unweariedly attentive to blow-by-blow accounts of endless single combats, whether of Achilles and Hector, Menelaus and Paris, or Arthur and Frollo, Lancelot and Meleagant.

Through love of a lady married to a king, Paris's passion for Menelaus' Helen, Lancelot's for Arthur's Guenevere, the fall of Troy and the destruction of the Round Table were accomplished. Priam, watching from the parapet as Achilles in his galloping quadriga drags the body of Hector around the walls of Troy, and Arthur, bending to catch the final words as Gawain's last blood seeps from wounds opened by Lancelot, are perennially heart-rending reminders of tragic human destiny.

Arthur's establishment of his right to the kingship by drawing his sword from the stone repeats the Theseus story—King Aegeus of Athens, when he begot the child at Troezen, left his sword under a boulder; when grown, the child, who alone could move the stone, took the sword and came to claim his heritage.

The Persephone myth has parallels in the abduction of Guenevere by Melwas/Meleagant, King of the Otherworld, and her rescue by

211

Arthur/Lancelot. A further counterpart is in one of the brief tales of Tristan and Iseult. Arthur arbitrates between Mark and Tristan, declaring she shall live with one during the season when the leaves are on the trees, and with the other in winter, with Mark to have first choice. But when he chooses winter, because the nights are longer, Iseult taunts him: the holly, the yew and the ivy, she says, never lose their leaves; she goes to Tristan forever.

Down the ages, there are parallels in the treatment as well as the content of the stories that attached themselves to the prehistoric Greek and the Dark Age British heroes. Both were transmitted by word of mouth for close to 500 years before they began to be written down. Thereafter, successive periods adapted the tales to their current moods and art forms, keeping the names but changing the presentation.

In classical Athens, Homer's poems supplied the plots of drama. Surviving texts present portrayals of the vengeance of Orestes by all three great playwrights of the Periclean Age, Aeschylus, Sophocles, Euripides, in styles that vary from the austerity of the beginning of the 5th century to the lyricism of its close. And the span from these tragedies to 19th century light opera in Offenbach's *La Belle Hélène* is strikingly similar to that from the medieval Arthurian romances to Lerner and Loewe's *Camelot*.

In the world of artifacts, too, shadowy relationships between the inhabitants of Britain and those of the Mediterranean tantalize modern curiosity. The peoples in Greece who in Minoan-Mycenaean times moved the great stones of Crete, Mycenae and Tiryns, and the peoples in Britain who moved the great stones of Avebury and Stonehenge and the menhirs of Brittany were contemporaries; those who came after them affirmed that the huge monoliths were set in place in the Age of Giants, and we know no more. Did the Giants know each other? How did the recently observed double-ax and dagger designs come to be carved on the Stonehenge sarsens at the height of the Minoan civilization when workmen carved similar designs on stones at the palaces of Crete?

Modern scholarship has yet to explain all that may have been conveyed by Diodorus of Sicily when in the 1st century B.C. he described Britain's temple to the Sun God:

In the regions beyond the land of the Celts there lies in the ocean an island no smaller than Sicily. This island . . . . is situated in the north and inhabited by the Hyperboreans, who are called by that name because their home is beyond the point whence the north wind (Boreas) blows; and the island is both fertile and productive of every crop, and since it has an unusually temperate climate it produces two harvests each year. Moreover, the following legend is told concerning it: Leto was born on this island, and for that reason Apollo is honoured among them above all other gods; and the inhabitants are looked upon as priests of Apollo, after a manner, since daily they praise this god continuously in song and honour him exceedingly. And there is also on the island both a magnificent sacred precinct of Apollo and a notable temple which is adorned with many votive offerings and is spherical in shape. . . . . .

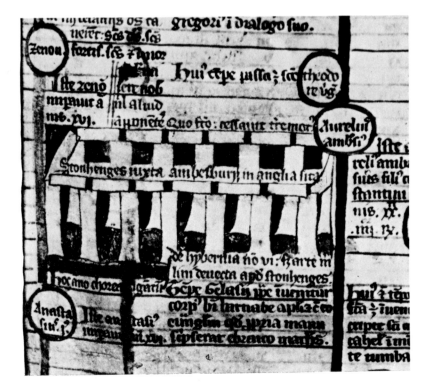

213

They say also that the moon, as viewed from this island, appears to be but a little distance from the earth, and to have upon it prominences, like those of the earth, which are visible to the eye. The account is also given that the god visits the island every 19 years, the period in which the return of the stars to the same place is accomplished. . . . . At the time of this appearance of the god he both plays on the cithara and dances continuously the night through from the vernal equinox to the rising of the Pleiades, expressing in this manner his delight in his successes. And the kings of this city and supervisors of the sacred precinct are called Boreales, since they are descendants of Boreas, and the succession to these positions is always kept in the family.

The Mediterranean amphorae shards of the 6th century A.D. that have been found on the hill called Camelot in Somerset witness a trade between the two regions that existed in Arthur's time. Was it continuous from the age when the peoples of the Eastern Mediterranean moved great plinths, and first used tin and copper to arm their fighting men with bronze?

The realm of Arthur that is currently being most intensively explored is a real realm; the findings of its explorers are giving historic depth to the most persistent myth of the Western heritage. With these new dimensions, the attraction of the Arthurian charisma continues, in a Western World burdened by the possibility of a cataclysmic last battle, and frustrated by plenty in a waste land.

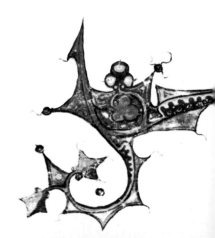

APPENDICES and INDEX

APPENDIX A

LIST OF ILLUSTRATIONS

Title	Liddington Hill Fort
9	South Cadbury Hill Fort
13	* Miniature of a hunt
14	* Miniature, lutanist before King Arthur
15	* Miniature, building of Caesar's ships
17	*** Page from *Four Ancient Books of Wales*
19	†† Detail from the Porta della Pescheria, Modena Cathedral
22	§ Ivory casket
23	† Miniature, Perlesvaus and the Maimed King hearing Mass
24	* Woodcut from Thomas East's 1585 reprint of Caxton's Malory
26	** Miniature, knights charging (Ashmole 828, f. 58)
27	† Miniature, castle of Morgan le Fay
29	Mosaic from Verulamium
32	* Initial G from MS of Caesar
33	* Battersea shield (left)
33	* British two-horned helmet (right)
35	Badge of the XX Legion
35	Fort at Rutupiae
36	Amphitheater, Verulamium
37	* Bust of Claudius
39	‡ Aerial view of Maiden Castle
39	Antler picks (permission of The National Trust)
40	Roman barracks at Caerleon
41	Icknield Way
43	Hadrian's Wall
44	Fort at Housesteads
45	Corbridge Supply Center
47	Stele from Colchester
49	‡ Detail of White Horse
49	‡ Coin found at Broadstairs
50	Silchester eagle (His Grace the Duke of Wellington's Silchester Collection, Reading Museum)
51	Caerwent walls
53	Head of Minerva (permission, Bath Museum)

THE REALMS OF ARTHUR

54	Mirror (permission, Shrewsbury Borough Museum)
55	Mosaic, Verulamium
56	* Bust found at Lullingstone Villa
56, 57	Mosaics, Bignor Villa
58	* Mildenhall plate, detail
59	‡ Wint Hill bowl
60	Celtic bowls (permission, Colchester Museum)
61	Charred mosaic (permission, Verulamium Museum)
62	§§§ Coins of Maximianus, Carausius, Allectus
63	Fortification walls, Portchester
63	* Coin of Constantius Chlorus
66	‡ Coin of Carausius
67	Silchester horse (His Grace the Duke of Wellington's Silchester Collection, Reading Museum)
72	* Impression, Sutton Hoo ship
73	* Buckle, Sutton Hoo
73	Longboat from a gravestone, Gotland, Sweden
74	* Grip extension from shield back (left), Sutton Hoo
74	* Ceremonial whetstone (right), Sutton Hoo
79	* Initial A from MS of Gildas
81	* Initial C from MS of Nennius
82	* Initial O from MS of the Venerable Bede
83	* Initial R from MS of William of Malmesbury
85	Cadbury Hill Fort
86	* Page from Leland
88	Slaughter Bridge
89	Inscribed stone near Slaughter Bridge
92	Badbury Rings
93	‡‡‡ Aerial view of Badbury Rings
94–95	‡ Aerial view of Uffington
97	Stream near Glastonbury
99	Eliseg's Pillar
104	Caer Gai
109	Tristan stone
112	Elan River below Cairn Cabal
113	Cairn Cabal
114	Arthur's Stone, Dore Valley
115	Arthur's Cave, Little Doward Hill
117	Castle ruins, Dinas Bran
118	*** Page from the *Black Book of Carmarthen*
123	Chepstow Castle

124   * Initial D from MS of Geoffrey of Monmouth

127   Oxford Castle

130   † Miniature, the begetting of Merlin (above)

130   * Miniature, Hengist slicing ox-hide (below)

131   * Miniature, Vortigern finds the red and white dragons (above)

131   ‡‡ Miniature, fight of the red and white dragons (below)

132   * Miniature, death of Vortigern; Vortigern and his courtiers

133   * Miniature, Merlin building Stonehenge

134   Avebury (above)

134   Stonehenge (below)

135   Grooved stone beside great trilithon, Stonehenge

137   Heelstone, Stonehenge

138   † Miniature, Merlin as a boy and Merlin carrying the Pendragon standard (top)

138   * Miniature, Uther sees Igerna (center)

138   * Miniature, Merlin and Uther in front of Tintagel Castle, Igerne inside (bottom)

139   Tintagel

140   * Miniature, the crowning of Arthur (above)

140   * Miniature, Arthur at Camelot (below)

141   * Miniature, Scots' ships surround island (above)

141   * Miniature, Arthur finds the Giant Ritho roasting a pig (below)

142–143   * Arthur's forces battle the Romans

144   * Miniature, the Round Table and the Last Battle (above)

144   * Miniature, Guenevere at the nunnery (below)

145   King Arthur, detail from tapestry (courtesy, The Metropolitan Museum of Art, The Cloisters Collection, Munsey Fund, 1932)

148   ** Manuscript border, detail of hunting (top) (Ashmole 828, f. 13^R)

148   * Miniature, assaulting a castle with a battering ram (center)

148   * Miniature, knights playing draughts (bottom)

149   * Illumined page, feast at Camelot

150   * Miniature, the victorious Arthur

151   Effigy of Robert Curthose, Gloucester Cathedral (above)

151   * Miniature, Galahad and Percival ride to a castle struck by lightning (below, left)

151   * Miniature, knights riding (below, right)

152   * Coats of Arms: Bleheris (left), Kay (right)

153   §§ The Round Table, Winchester Castle

154–155   § Tapestry (left to right): Tristan kills a dragon; Mark's servant gets the dragon's head; servant brings the head to King Mark

156   § Ivory casket, the tryst beneath the tree (right-hand half of carving)

219

157   § Sicilian bed quilt, with Tristan story

158   † Miniature, Arthur enthroned, center; the Queen and Lancelot, right (above)

158   † Miniature, the Horn of Chastity (below)

159   § Ivory casket, Lancelot on the Sword Bridge

160   * Miniature, Elaine of Astolat (above)

160   ††† Miniature, Lancelot and Guenevere's first kiss (below)

161   ** Miniature, Lancelot comes to the hermitage (Douce 215, f. 14)

162   † Miniature, combat of Gawain and Lancelot

163   * Miniature, Galahad and Percival find the white stag (above)

163   * Miniatures, The Grail (below)

164   * Miniature, Galahad's sword in the stone

165   Glastonbury Tor

169   Site of lake village, on left

170   Lake village bowl, Glastonbury Museum

171   Glastonbury Tor from the marsh

174   St. Mary's Chapel, Glastonbury

175   Glastonbury Abbey ruins

180   Abbot's Kitchen (left)

180   Abbot's Barn (center)

181   Abbot's Fish House

182   The Tribunal, Glastonbury

182   Dozmary Pool

183   Miniature, Arthur sails to Avalon (Biblioteca Nationale Centrale Firenze)

184   * Miniature, the Last Battle

185   * Miniature, Joseph collecting Blood and Sweat in cruets (above)

185   *** The Nanteos Cup (below)

186   Abbot Bere's device in stone

187   Abbot Bere's device in glass

188   Priest at Muchelney (left)

188   Joseph on Plymtree rood screen (right)

191   Ancient tree at Burnham Beeches

194   * Miniature, King Henry dictating (above)

194   † Miniature, the Grail Procession (below)

196   * Miniature, the Green Knight holding his head

197   Carved detail from Dieulacres Abbey, inserted in barn

198   The Roaches in storm

199   Lud's church—the Green Chapel

204   * Uther and Ygerne, woodcut from Caxton's *Morte Darthur*

205   † Miniature, Galahad knighted, from a MS that belonged to Jacques
        d'Armagnac, dated 1463

206   ** Miniature, death of Guenevere (Ashmole 828, f. 43v)

207   Lancelot and the dragon, woodcuts from Caxton's *Morte Darthur*

209   Stonehenge, detail of dagger

213   **** Earliest portrayal of Stonehenge in an English MS

215   ** Manuscript border (Douce 215, f. 1^R)

    *   courtesy, Trustees of the British Museum

    **   courtesy, the Bodleian Library

   ***   courtesy, the National Library of Wales, Aberystwyth

****   courtesy, The Masters and Fellows of Corpus Christi College,
    Cambridge

    §   courtesy, the Victoria and Albert Museum

   §§   courtesy, photograph the British Travel Association

    ‡   courtesy, photograph the Ashmolean Museum

   ‡‡   courtesy, The Archbishop of Canterbury and the Trustees of Lambeth
    Palace Library

  ‡‡‡   courtesy, Aerofilms, Ltd.

    †   courtesy, Bibliothèque Nationale Française

   ††   courtesy, photograph The Metroplitan Museum of Art

  †††   courtesy, The Pierpont Morgan Library

 §§§   courtesy, American Numismatic Society

all other photographs by the author

Longboat on page 173 reproduced by permission of Dr. Gunnar
Svahnström

MAPS

page

 31   The Realm of Roman Britannia

 69   The Realm of the Great Battle

101   The Realm of the Celtic West

125   The Realm of Pseudo-History

147   The Realm of Never-Never Land

167   The Realm of Avalon

193   The Realm of the Repatriated Legends

APPENDIX B

Sources of quotations not identified in the text:

Page

13   Bodel, Jean *La Chanson des Saxons*

19   William of Malmesbury *Acts of the Kings of England*
    Hearne, Thomas *A History of the Antiquities of Glastonbury*

21   Geoffrey of Monmouth *History of the Kings of Britain*

25   Hanford, James Holly *A Milton Handbook*
    Milton, John *Paradise Lost,* Book IX

32   Caesar, C. Julius *Conquest of Gaul* (trans. S. A. Hanford)

33   Caesar, C. Julius op. cit.

42   Tacitus *Agricola*

48   Tacitus op. cit.

52   Caesar, C. Julius op. cit.
    Tacitus op. cit.

64   Procopius *History of the Wars*

65   Chambers, R. W. *England Before the Norman Conquest*

68   Baring-Gould, S. & Fisher, John *Lives of the British Saints*

71   Gildas *The Loss and Conquest of Britain*

76   Procopius op. cit.

87   Antiquarians' Journal, vol. XLVIII, part I, 1968

96   Gildas op. cit.

103   Bromwich, Rachel (trans.) *The Welsh Triads*

105   *Pa Gur*

106   Jones, Gwyn & Thomas (trans.) *The Mabinogion*

110   Jarrett, Michael G. & Dobson, Brian, eds. *Britain and Rome*

119   Dillon, Myles & Chadwick, Nora *The Celtic Realms*
    Jones, Gwyn & Thomas op. cit.

120   Jones, Gwyn & Thomas op. cit.

129   William of Malmesbury op. cit.

144   Brengle, Richard *Arthur, King of Britain,* excerpt from *Le Morte Arthur* *

152   Chambers, E. K. *Arthur of Britain,* excerpt from Wace's *Brut*

* *Arthur King of Britain,* History, Romance, Chronicle, & Criticism, with texts in modern English, from Gildas to Malory. Edited by Richard L. Brengle. Copyright © 1964 by Meredith Publishing Company. Reprinted by permission of Appleton-Century-Crofts.

154   Loomis, R. S. *Arthurian Legends in Mediaeval Art*

161   Evans, Sebastian *High History of the Holy Grail*

167   Powicke, F. M., trans. Walter Daniels *Life of Ailred of Rievaulx*

172   anon. *History and Antiquities of Glastonbury* (1794)

175   Butler, H. E. (trans.) *Autobiography of Giraldus Cambrensis*

177   Hunt, Robert *Popular Romances of the West of England*

Chambers, E. K. op. cit.

Leland, John *Assertio Inclytissimi Arthurij Britanniae*

178–180   Stokes, H. F. Scott, trans. *William of Malmesbury's On the Antiquity of the Church of Glastonbury*

190   Evans, Sebastian op. cit.

193   Trevelyan, G. M. *History of England*

194   Brengle, Richard op. cit.

197   Boroff, Marie (trans.) *Sir Gawain and the Green Knight*

213   Diodorus Siculus *Bibliotheca Historica*

APPENDIX C

BRIEF BIBLIOGRAPHY

The pursuit of Arthur can be begun from many points of departure. A start can be made with the general summaries of what is known about him and about the legends that cluster around his name. Pertinent background and quoted selections, in modern English, from both near-contemporary chronicles and medieval romances are compactly contained in E. K. Chambers' *Arthur of Britain,* Cambridge, 1927, reprinted with supplementary bibliography in 1965, and Richard L. Brengle's *King Arthur of Britain,* Appleton-Century-Crofts, New York, 1964. The former places its quoted material in a setting as comprehensive as a general reader is apt to need; the latter collects illuminating passages from the 6th-to-9th century writings of the Celtic monks Gildas and Nennius through the early 12th century pseudo-history in which Geoffrey of Monmouth combined fact and fancy to the late 12th–15th century avowed romances of the Continental poets and the English version of the entire Arthurian cycle written by Sir Thomas Malory at the end of the medieval period.

Complete texts of the chief chronicles and romances are readily available, most of them in portable form convenient for travelling readers who intend to visit sites. Penguin offers Lewis Thorpe's recent translation (1966) of *Geoffrey of Monmouth's History of the Kings of Britain.* Everyman provides early Welsh stories of Arthur in Gwyn Jones' and Thomas Jones' translation of *The Mabinogion* (No. 97), the accounts of the Anglo-Norman Wace and the English Layamon in *Arthurian Chronicles* (No. 578), poems written at the Angevin court, *The Lays of Marie de France* (No. 557), tales of the French romancer-in-chief, Chrétien de Troyes, *Arthurian Romances* (No. 698) and Malory's English version of the Arthurian cycle, *Le Morte d'Arthur* (Nos. 45–46).

The numerous books written or edited by R. S. Loomis consider Arthurian problems and present discussions and translations of the stories; among them, *Arthurian Literature in the Middle Ages,* Oxford, 1959, and *The Development of Arthurian Romance,* 1963; his profusely illustrated *Arthurian Legends in Medieval Art,* 1938, brings illumined manuscripts, tapestries, frescoes and carvings within the view of the armchair reader and signals their present location to the person preparing to travel.

For the motorist, the cyclist or the walker, an exceptional series of British maps makes route-planning an anticipatory pleasure. Bartholomew's ten-miles-to-the-inch modern county map of England and Wales begins his orientation; he can overlay it on the Ordnance Survey's map of *Roman Britain, Britain in the Dark Ages,* and *Ancient Britain* —the two sheets, North and South, of the last of these locate all antiquities older than 1066 A.D. Once an overall itinerary is decided, the pertinent sections, available separately, of the National Grid inch-to-the-mile series bring into enlarged focus the sites that are less easy to find and show not only roads but footpaths.

THE REALMS OF ARTHUR

Country Life, Ltd. publishes *Ancient Monuments Open to the Public,* a check-list giving locations, times when open, and admission where charged; the Ministry of Works issues (free with a season ticket) a similar list of *Ancient Monuments and Historic Buildings* that are in its care.

At all major and many minor sites, accurate and lucid pamphlets, with diagrams, prepared by ranking authorities as official guides for the Ministry of Works, publications of local historical societies, and museum catalogues document both the history of the place and the significance of ruins or artifacts remaining. The British Museum's pamphlet series gives separate treatment to the artifacts from major finds or excavations on view in its exhibition halls—the Sutton Hoo ship burial, the Mildenhall treasure, and general surveys, such as its *Guide to the Antiquities of Roman Britain, Roman Forts of the Saxon Shore,* etc.; the National Museum of Wales not only documents its display cases item by item but produces such publications as *Isca, Roman Caerleon.* Smaller museum guides from Colchester and St. Albans to Salisbury and Shrewsbury, pamphlets of city archivist offices such as Coventry's *Guide to St. Mary's Hall,* shire publications such as *Discovering Wiltshire* can be picked up on the spot. For evening reading, an historical novel which embodies much history and archaeological research regarding Arthur is Rosemary Sutcliff's *Sword at Sunset.* Current reports on archaeological investigation at traditional Arthurian sites and a review of the legends are available in *The Quest for Arthur's Britain,* edited and in part written by Geoffrey Ashe, with chapters by Leslie Alcock, C. A. Ralegh Radford, Philip Rahtz and Jill Racy, 1968.

For the serious student, particularly of medieval romance, the milepost zero in a pursuit of Arthur in his kingly form is the Manuscript Room of the British Museum; he will find it difficult to get away from the post. (Even the casual traveller will pore over the illumined treasures from this collection—such as the unique copy of Sir Gawain and the Green Knight—displayed in the Museum's exhibit halls.) Once having entered the period of the Angevin kings of Britain, the student will be tempted to cross the Channel to their majesties' French holdings and lose himself again in Paris in the Bibliothèque Nationale, whose wealth ranges from the first known illumined manuscript to the opulent magnificence of the remaining three-quarters of the 1100 folios comprising the entire Arthurian cycle, prepared in the 1460's for Jacques d'Armagnac, duc de Nemours.

Individual items of importance can be found in the university libraries and the libraries of the component colleges Oxford and Cambridge, the Lambeth Palace Library, the National Library of Wales at Aberystwyth, the Widener at Harvard and the Morgan Collection in New York.

As suggestions related to specific aspects of the Arthurian story not mentioned above, the following very brief lists have been compiled, chapter by chapter.

CHAPTER II

BIRLEY, E., *Roman Britain and the Roman Army,* Wilson and Son, Kendal, 1961

BLAIR, PETER HUNTER, *Roman Britain and Early England, 55 B.C.–A.D. 871,* Nelson, Edinburgh, 1963

COLLINGWOOD, R. G. and MYRES, J. N. L., *Roman Britain and the English Settlements,* 2nd ed., Oxford, 1937

COTTRELL, LEONARD, *Seeing Roman Britain,* Evans, London, 1956

KENDRICK, SIR THOMAS, *British Antiquity,* Methuen, London, 1950

RICHMOND, I. A., *Roman Britain,* Cape, London, 1963

CHAPTER III

BARBER, RICHARD W., *Arthur of Albion,* Barrie & Rockliff, London, 1961

CARADOC OF LLANCARFAN, *Life of Gildas,* Lives of the British Saints, S. Baring-Gould and John Fisher, eds. Cymmrodion Society, London, 1911

CHADWICK, H. M., *Origin of the English Nation,* Cambridge, 1907

CHADWICK, NORA K., ed., *Studies in Early British History,* Cambridge, 1954

CRAWFORD, O. G. S., and KEILLER, ALEXANDER, *Wessex from the Air,* Oxford University Press, 1938

GILES, J. A., ed. & trans., *Six Old English Chroniclers,* Bohn's Antiquarian Library, London, 1848

JACKSON, KENNETH, *Language and History in Early Britain,* Edinburgh University Press, 1953

MITFORD, R. L. S. BRUCE, *The Sutton Hoo Ship Burial,* British Museum, 1947

MORRIS, JOHN R., *The Age of Arthur,* a history of Great Britain from A.D. 350 to A.D. 650 (forthcoming)

SCUDDER, VIDA D., ed., *The Ecclesiastical History of the English Nation by the Venerable Bede,* J. M. Dent & Sons, London & Toronto, 1930

SHARPE, J., trans., *William of Malmesbury's Acts of the Kings of England, 1854*

WADE-EVANS, A. W., trans., *Nennius' History of the Britons,* Society for Promoting Christian Knowledge, London, 1938

WHITELOCK, DOROTHY, ed. & trans., *The Anglo-Saxon Chronicle,* Eyre & Spottiswoode, London, 1961

WRIGHT, D., trans., *Beowulf,* Penguin, London, 1957

THE REALMS OF ARTHUR

CHAPTER IV

BROMWICH, RACHEL, ed. & trans., *Trioedd Ynys Prydein* (The Welsh Triads), University of Wales, Cardiff, 1961

CHADWICK, NORA K., *The Age of the Saints in the Early Celtic Church,* Oxford, 1961, reprinted, 1963

DILLON, MYLES and CHADWICK, NORA, *The Celtic Realms,* Weidenfeld & Nicolson, London, 1967

SKENE, WILLIAM D., *The Four Ancient Books of Wales* (2 vols.) Edinburgh, 1868

WILLIAMS, GWYN, ed., *Presenting Welsh Poetry, an Anthology of Welsh Verse in Translation and of English Verse by Welsh Poets,* Faber, London, 1959

CHAPTER V

NEWALL, R. S. *Stonehenge,* Ministry of Works, H. M. Stationery Office, London, 1959

HAWKINS, GERALD S. and WHITE, J. B., *Stonehenge Decoded,* Souvenir Press, 1966

CHAPTER VI

BRUCE, JAMES DOUGLAS, *Evolution of Arthurian Romance from the Beginnings Down to the Year 1300,* Peter Smith, Gloucester, Mass., 1958, (Johns Hopkins Press, 1928)

CHAMBERS, SIR E. K., *English Literature at the Close of the Middle Ages,* Oxford, 1947

CHAPTER VII

ASHE, GEOFFREY, *King Arthur's Avalon,* Collins, London, 1957, repr. 1963

BUTLER, H. E., trans., *The Autobiography of Giraldus Cambrensis,* Cape, London, 1937

HEARNE, THOMAS, trans., *John of Glastonbury's Chronicle, 1726; Adam of Domersham's Chronicle, 1727*

ROBINSON, J. ARMITAGE, *Two Glastonbury Legends: King Arthur and St. Joseph of Arimathea,* Cambridge University Press, 1926

STOKES, H. F. SCOTT, trans., William of Malmesbury's *On the Antiquity of the Church of Glastonbury,* based on the unique manuscript in the Library of Trinity College, Cambridge. "Central Somerset Gazette", Glastonbury, 1932

TREHARNE, R. F., *The Glastonbury Legends,* Cresset, London, 1967

WARNER, RICHARD, *An History of the Abbey of Glastonbury; and of the Town of Glastonbury,* Crittwell, Bath, 1826

CHAPTER VIII

BOROFF, MARIE, trans., *Sir Gawain and the Green Knight* (alliterative verse) Norton, N.Y., 1967

ELLIOTT, RALPH W. V., *A Detective Essay in Literary Geography, The Times,* London, May 21, 1958

EVANS, SEBASTIAN, trans., *The High History of the Holy Grail* (Perlesvaus), Dent, London, 1899

FISHER, MICHAEL J. E., *History of Dieulacres Abbey,* M.A. thesis, University of Keele, 1967

HICKS, E., *Sir Thomas Malory, His Turbulent Career,* Oxford University Press, 1928

MATTHEWS, WILLIAM, *The Ill-framed Knight, a Skeptical Inquiry into the Identity of Sir Thomas Malory,* Cambridge University Press, 1967

VINAVER, EUGENE, ed., *The Works of Sir Thomas Malory,* (3 vols.) Oxford University Press, 1947

INDEX

A

Agricola   16, 42, 48

Ailred of Rievaulx   166–167

Alcock, Leslie   87.

Alcuin   130

Ambrosius Aurelianus (Aurelius Ambrosius)   80–83, 90, 125, 130–133, 137, 140

Amesbury   81, 140, 144, 206

Anglo-Saxon Chronicle   16, 65, 70, 78, 92, 96, 110

Arthur   12ff, 19, 28, 44, 104, 105, 214

   and Bran   116–118

   as a Worthy   14, 154

   at south Cadbury (Camelot)   85–87

   battle of Badon   80, 82, 90, 92–98, 195

   blazon   150–151

   conquests   140–142, 211

   crowned   140

   dog Cabal   113–114

   first mention of, by Nennius   81

   graves at Glastonbury   174–179

   his armor   150–151

   his battles   81–82, 90–91

   his passing   20, 183–184

   his ship Prydwen   20, 119

   in *Culhwch and Olwen*   119

   in *Dream of Rhonabwy*   119

   in Geoffrey of Monmouth   ch. v passim

   in *Gododdin*   91

   in lament for Geraint   110

   in *Pa Gur*   105–106

   in romances   157–158

   in the lives of the saints   168

   in Welsh triads   107, 118, 125

   last battle   83, 88–92, 143, 211

   marries Guenevere   141

   places named for   18

   Pomparles Bridge   182

   Ritho the Giant   142

   Round Table 13, 23, 25, 152–154, 161, 164, 211

   siring of Modred   158, 194–195

   sites of courts   107, 141

   sons of   111

   sword in the stone   23, 211

   the name   82, 126, 154

Arthur's Cave   115–116, 132

   Grave   116

   Oven   89, 114

   Stone   114

Avalon   22, 168, 173, 176, 177, 179, 180, 183

B

Badbury Rings   38, 92, 93

Badon, Battle of (Mons Badonicus)   15, 80, 90, 92–98, 141, 150

Bale, John   177, 200
Bath-Hill   80, 93, 141, 195
Bede, the Venerable   17, 82, 124, 128
Bedivere (Bedwyr)   105–107
Beowulf   72–75, 194
Biket, Robert   158
Blair, Peter Hunter   96–97
Blazons of Round Table Knights   150–152
    of Abbot Bere of Glastonbury   186–187
Bleheris   121, 152
Bodel, Jean   12–13, 15, 20–21
Bretons   18, 26
Brittany   19
Bruts, histories of England   23, 195
Brutus, England's first king   21, 23

C

Caerleon   40, 50, 91, 128, 141, 144, 158, 179
Caesar, C. Julius   15, 30, 32ff, 52
Camelot   11–12, 15, 25, 84ff, 214
Camlann   15, 83, 88–90, 126, 143, 178–179, 183
Camulodunum (Colchester)   34, 36, 50, 59
Caradoc of Llancarfan   68–70, 168
Castle Dore   108–109
Catraeth, battle of   91
Caxton, William   24, 154, 202–208
Chrétien de Troyes   23, 122, 148, 159, 172
Claudius   16, 34, 36
Cogidubnus, king of the Regenses   37–38
Commius, king of the Atrebates   32, 34
Culhwch and Olwen   106–107, 119

D

Dieulacres Abbey   196–197
Dinas Bran   116, 189
Diodorus Siculus   213
Dozmary Pool   182
Dream of Macsen Wledig   103
Dream of Rhonabwy   119–120
Druids   51–52

E

Eleanor of Aquitaine   18, 22, 121, 146
Eliseg, Pillar of   103
Emperors (Roman) in Britain
    Alectus, usurper   62
    Antoninus Pius   44
    Caesar   15, 32–34, 52
    Caracalla   45
    Carausius, usurper   62
    Hadrian   43
    Honorius   65
    Constantinus III, usurper   64–65, 130
    Constantius Chlorus   62
    Maximus, Magnus Clemens   64, 103
    Theodosius I   64
    Vespasian   38

F

Four Ancient Books of Wales   17
Frere, Sheppard   90–91

G

Galahad   23, 151, 160, 164

Gawain (Gwalchmei) 19, 104–105, 142, 151, 156, 158–162, 195, 200, 211

Geoffrey of Monmouth 18, 20, 21, ch. v passim, 133, 137–144, 150, 161, 208

Geraint (Gereint) 109–111

Gerald of Wales (see Giraldus Cambrensis)

Germanus 77

Gibbon, Edward 75

Gildas' *Loss and Conquest of Britain* 17, 25, 60, 71, 79–80, 90, 96, 124, 128, 129–130, 168, 200

Giraldus Cambrensis 128–129, 175–177

Glastonbury 22, 25, 164–190, ch. vii passim
  chief monastic building 169, 180–181
  derivation of name 172–173
  thorn 188–189
  Tor 171–172, 180, 186

Grail, the Holy 20, 22, 23, 162–164, 185–187

Grey, Lady Jane 150

Guenevere (Guinevere, Gwenhwyfar, Winlogee) 19, 22, 111, 141, 142, 144, 159–161, 174, 176–178, 206–207, 211

H

Hadrian's Wall 43–44, 90, 91

Hardyng, John 153

Helinand de Froidmont 162

Henry I 129, 140

Henry II 121, 122, 126, 127, 140, 148, 173, 175, 176, 192

Henry III 21, 154

Henry of Huntington 18, 128

Herman of Tournai 114

Hill forts 38–40
  see also Iron Age forts

Holinshed's *Chronicles* 24–25

I

Icknield Way 41, 93, 96

Iron Age Forts
  Badbury 93
  Badbury Rings 38, 92, 94
  Barbury 95
  Hambledon 40
  Hod 40
  Liddington 93–95
  Maiden 38
  Solsbury 90

J

Jacques de Longuyon 14

Joseph of Arimathea 22, 162–164, 173, 184–189
  his chalice 22, 185–186
  his cruets 22, 185–187
  his thorn and staff 187–189
  in chronicles 162–163, 173, 185
  in West Country legends 185

K

Kay (Kei, Cei) 19, 105–107, 152, 159

L

Lake villages in Somerset 169–170

Lancelot (Launcelot) 23, 151–152, 159–162, 190, 202, 206, 211

Layamon   183, 195
Legions (Roman) in Britain   34, 38,
   43, 46–48, 61, 64, 76
Leland, John   84–86, 88–89, 177–178,
   200
Liddington   93–95

M

Mabinogion   102, 103, 119, 120
Maimed King, the   11, 20, 163, 194
Malory, Sir Thomas   24, 154, 200–208
Map, Walter   192
Marie de Champagne   22, 146–148
Marie de France   24
Mark, King of Cornwall   107–109
Matter of Britain   12–13, 15
Matthews, William   202 ff
Melwas (Meleagant)   159, 168, 172–
   180, 211
Merlin   12, 18, 20, 126, 131, 132–133,
   203
Milton, John   25
Morgan le Fay   20
Modred (Medrault)   19, 83, 89, 141–
   143, 162, 178–179, 194
Morris, John R.   98, 211
Morte Arthure   183–184, 203
Morte Darthur   24, 154, 200–208

N

Nanteos Cup   185–186
Nennius' *History of the Britons*   17,
   81–82, 111–113, 124, 128, 151
Nine Worthies   14, 154

O

Offa's Dyke   128

P

Pelagius   77
Percival (Perlesvaus, Peredur, Perceval,
   Parsifal)   11, 111, 161, 163, 189–
   190, 194
Portchester (Llongborth)   62, 110
Procopius   64, 76, 96

R

Robert Curthose   151
Robert, Earl of Gloucester   129
Robert de Boron   23, 164
Romano-British villas   54 ff
Round Table, the   13, 23, 25, 152–154,
   161, 164, 211
Ruben of Bath   177
Rutupiae   34, 62, 142

S

Sir Gawain and the Green Knight   105,
   195–200
Siege Perilous, the   23, 153, 164
South Cadbury hill fort   15, 25, 84–87,
   171–172, 214
St. Germanus   77
Stephen, King   21, 127, 129
Stevens, C. E.   96
Stonehenge   132–137, 212–214
Stukeley   85

Sutton Hoo Ship Burial   71–74
Swindon Gap   92–94
Sword in the stone   23, 211

T

Tacitus   15, 42, 48–49, 52
Tintagel   138–139, 172, 189, 190, 204
Twrch Trwynt   118, 211
Trimontium (Newstead)   42, 76
Tribal capitals, Romano-British   48–54
Tristan, Iseult and Mark   107–109,
    152, 155–156, 160, 212

U

Uther Pendragon   105, 126, 130, 132,
    137–140, 203

V

Verulamium (St. Albans)   36, 50, 59
Vinaver, Eugène   202
Vortigern   77–78, 80, 90, 103, 118,
    130–132

Vortimer   81, 83

W

Wace, Maistre   23, 126, 195
Wansdyke   92–93
Welsh literature
    bards   17, 100–102
    Mabinogion   102, 119
    Pa Gur   105
    storytellers   17
    Triads   ch. iv passim, 17, 102, 107,
    111, 116–118, 125, 180
White Horse   49
William of Malmesbury   18, 19, 83,
    105, 128, 151
    pseudo-William   178–180
Winchester   25, 27, 153
Wolfram von Eschenbach   163

Z

Zosimus   65